Choosing Comedy
Scenes from God's Sitcom

by
Robin Troia Schmidt

Choosing Comedy: Scenes from God's Sitcom
Copyright © 2019 by Robin Troia Schmidt

Some of these essays first appeared in the author's blog choosingcomedy.com between 2007 and 2018.

Cover design: Allison Weyand and Robin Troia Schmidt.

Cover Photo Credits: Allison Weyand, "Shoes and Hose", "Eiffel Tower", "Wrist Tattoo", author portrait

All other photos: Robin Troia Schmidt

ISBN: 9781691702558

CHOOSING COMEDY

Dedication

For Anne, Michael and Allison.

You three are my heart. I have grown up in God alongside you, so I wasn't always good at pointing God out to you. More often, God showed me himself through you.

I love you.

Contents

Foreword

When my children were young, we used to pass the time on long car trips by playing the game, "I Spy." At first, the things we "spied" were easily spotted, but as the kids grew, we made the objects more difficult to identify, requiring more patience and a keener eye.

Eventually they got too old for what they dubbed a kid's game, so we stopped playing altogether. I can't help but think this is how we relate to God. When we're young, he's easy to spot, but as we grow older, he's more difficult to find, until finally we just stop looking.

Noticing where God intersects with our lives is difficult because we're busy, distracted, and often in a hurry to get things done.

I recently walked right past a good friend in the grocery store because I was so focused on finding the items my wife needed for a new recipe.

God is often similarly unseen or unnoticed, usually because there are a myriad of other things vying for our attention. It's easy to recognize how God was watching out for us when a big calamity is averted. But what about the stuff of ordinary life? Surely God isn't just waiting for disaster to strike before he intervenes?

He's not.

He's always on the job, and we are always in need of someone pointing this out to us, just like Robin does in this wonderful little book. Whether it's driving to work, potty training a child, or mopping up a flooded basement, she shows us that God is not only aware, but intimately involved in all of it.

Sometimes he's teaching us a lesson, while other times he just wants us to laugh and not take ourselves so seriously. Mostly he is showing and telling us that he loves us more than we can imagine.

As a pastor I'm always on the lookout for where our stories connect with God's, so I am grateful for the many examples in this book. Even though I knew many of these stories (I was even present for some) before they were in print, it's important to hear them again and again. Because I am a forgetful person, part of a human race that is also forgetful, and we all need to be reminded of who we are and whose we are.

Reverend Douglas H. Walker
River City Church, EPC
DeBary, FL

(formerly of Grace Chapel, EPC
Farmington Hills, MI)

CHOOSING COMEDY

Preface

According to family history my first sentence was: "I read a book." I was in the bathtub holding a partially submerged Reader's Digest when I made this declarative statement.

It was not only a childhood milestone, but greatly prophetic. This is what I love to do. I read books.

I also love to laugh. And there was a lot of laughter in my house growing up. We enjoyed listening to classic comedians on the turntable. We joked and teased one another.

Laughter was not without its hazards, however. Growing up, more often than not, if I laughed hard, like really hard, well...I'd wet my pants. That made for a lot of embarrassing moments. But it did not deter me. A good laugh was worth a little embarrassment.

I value a good sense of humor.

That's what attracted me to my husband. His sense of humor. Very few people can make me laugh as easily and heartily as he can. And there has been a lot of laughter (and a few puddles) in our house as we raised our family.

Early in our marriage my husband sought out a bookstore to purchase a birthday present for me. I was delighted with the book he gave me and asked him how he selected it. He told me he went for the thickest book, so it would last longer.

We moved eight times in our first eight years of marriage, and one of my brothers helped with almost every move. In the midst of one move he looked at me from under a large box of books and said, "You people read too much."

I learned to pack the books in smaller boxes.

Laughter, as it turns out, was more than what attracted me to my husband. More than the thing that left me damp if indulged to excess.

Laughter was a lifeline.

Seeing humor in a situation, laughing at myself, was the buoy that kept me afloat when the darkness of depression threatened to pull me under.

For a long time, I didn't know I suffered from depression. And humor kept people around me from knowing too.

When circumstances went crazy wrong, I stepped outside of myself and watched it like an audience, as though it was a situation comedy. So much so that I started to think maybe I was starring in God's favorite situation comedy.

It became a philosophy: keep your sense of humor and you're in a sitcom, lose your sense of humor and you're stuck in the drama. And who needs any more drama?

I would relay the humor of our daily lives to friends and family, first in letters, then in emails. Stringing words together, coming up with the right turn of a phrase can be so satisfying, especially if it invokes a reaction from others...laughter, thoughtfulness, tears.

People who loved me frequently encouraged me to write more, write a book. But I didn't think I had anything to say.

I liked the idea of being in a sitcom though. In my mind comedy equaled laughter. You may imagine my disappointment when I rented a movie from the library in the category "comedy" and found it was not funny at all.

I don't mean that I had a different sense of humor than the writers, I mean it wasn't humorous. They didn't seem to be going for laughs.

Wanting to know how a movie that didn't evoke laughter could be labeled a comedy, I headed to Google and stumbled upon some introductory lecture notes from Professor Ian Johnston's Studies in Shakespeare course.[1] From his notes I got a deeper understanding of the category "comedy" and its relation, not to drama, but to tragedy.

According to Professor Johnston while all stories involve conflict, the dramatic structures of comedy and tragedy are defined by the way the people in a story approach and react to the conflict of the story. Whether someone's story is a comedy or tragedy depends largely on the choices they make.

As I read, I couldn't help but think how this sounded so much like the overarching story we are all in: Life.

God's story.

The story begins in harmony. Community is enjoyed by God, a man and a woman.

Humpty Dumpty sat on a wall.

But something happens. The conflict occurs. The man and woman listen to a voice other than God's. They choose to trust this new voice instead of trusting God. This upsets the relationships of all involved.

Humpty Dumpty Had a Great Fall.

The man and woman have broken their relationship with
God. They trusted another voice, not his, did what they
wanted, not what he told them to do.

We, coming after them, are born into this fallen, broken state
of relationship to God, in a now fallen and broken world.

How do we deal with this broken world? How do we get back
what was lost: the unity, the community we enjoyed with God
before the fall?

In both comedies and tragedies, the characters will work to
restore the community, work to resolve the conflict.

All the King's Horses and All the King's Men.

Humpty gets help from all the king's horses and all the king's
men. They are valiant in their attempt to piece him back
together. But sadly, they...

Couldn't Put Humpty Together Again.

In a tragedy, according to Professor Johnston, the main
character "desires to confront the world on his own terms, to
get the world to answer to (him)."[2] The tragic figure is
"increasingly persuaded that he can deal with what is
happening only on his own."[3]

If we attempt to address our brokenness on our own terms,
convinced that we and we alone can solve it, our story will
end like the scrambled egg, in failure.

By contrast, in a comedy, the main characters learn some

important lesson, about life and about themselves, before the conflict is resolved.

If our lives are a comedy, we will learn the most important lesson: *We* can't fix it.

We can't. The king's horses and men couldn't fix it.

But what about the King?

Jesus, the Son of God, entered our story to address the conflict we cannot resolve. He took our place, suffered the consequences of our disobedience. He died in our place.

But he didn't remain dead. He resurrected. He offers us, through himself, a way to successfully restore community, to restore our relationship with God. He did what we could not do for ourselves.

If you are familiar at all with Jesus, you know that he invited people to follow him.

Except one time.

One time a man specifically asked for permission to follow Jesus, actually, he begged to be allowed to go with him.[4]

And to this one man, Jesus said, No.

No? Really? Why?

Jesus healed this man, gave him his life back. In gratitude and awe the man begs to be allowed to go with him. And Jesus said, No.

No, instead, go home and tell people what God has done for you.

Tell people what God has done for you.

In this book I am telling you, with stories and metaphors and analogies, what I understand about God and what he has done for me.

I don't *fully* understand God, nor do I understand everything he has done for me. But I will share what I have. I will share my handful of pieces that belong to a puzzle that is so much larger than me, that the very idea of how small my pieces are in the big picture is rather incomprehensible to me.

But I think this is everyone's burden when they have encountered God. Go home and tell what God has done for you.

Will everyone listen? Not necessarily.

But I am only responsible for my choices. God has done much for me, so it is my burden, my responsibility, to tell it.[5]

What follows is some of my story. These are pictures God has painted on the canvas of my mind. They are some of the pieces of his puzzle that he has entrusted to me.

I share them with you. Little pieces. Like scenes from God's sitcom.

And I invite you to consider the choice that is before each of us: Which will my life be? The tragedy or the comedy?

Address the major issue of life on my own, and fail? Or accept that Jesus has addressed it for me, and live?

CHOOSING COMEDY

Humpty Dumpty Had a Great Fall

CHOOSING COMEDY

"Everything will be all right in the end. If it's not all right, it is not yet the end."

Sonny Kapoor,
Best Exotic Marigold Hotel[6]

Answers

I have complete confidence that there is an answer for everything.

The difficulty comes in because I want that answer.

When my oldest was in 7th grade, she came to me with her math book and said, "I don't understand how to answer this question." A problem was posed, and she needed to give an answer, not a numerical answer, but an answer that showed she understood the process of what they were asking.

Trouble was she didn't understand. And neither did I.

The directions were very specific. You are not to use a calculator.

Huh.

So, I reached for a calculator.

My eldest freaked.

"The Directions say DO NOT USE A CALCULATOR!!!!!!!!"

"I know," I answered. "And *you* will not use one. I, on the other hand, must use a calculator to understand what they are asking so that I can then explain it to you."

I couldn't get there myself, I needed the calculator. Eventually I would understand the concept well enough that I could get there myself. But not at first.

I approach life in a similar way.

There is an answer. I may not be able to get there on my own.

Yet.

Still, I want to know the answer as I make my way through the problem.

When I was in the hospital giving birth to my second child I was moving around a lot. Actually, I was bouncing around on the bed.

My doctor asked me, "What are you doing?"

I said, "I am trying to get comfortable."

With the wisdom of Solomon, he responded, "You won't be comfortable until it is over."

But I want to be comfortable right *now*. And what would make me comfortable? Knowing everything is going to be all right in the end.

When I read other people's stories in the Bible I don't have to wait for the ending. In just a few pages, maybe even just a few verses, the end of the story comes.

This is almost worse than TV, where every problem is resolved within 30 to 60 minutes. I become conditioned. I expect to know the end right now.

Yet, as a woman I recognize that some of the middle stuff is being left out of the Bible. I am not reading in "real" time. When I read, "and Leah begot Reuben" I realize there is a lot more to it than the word "begot."

I would like to skip past the middle stuff in my life too. I want to know the end of the story, now. *Now*, before the end.

I will be able to relax and enjoy life if I know everything is going to be all right in the end.

Reading Job's story I can reflect and glean truth from it, knowing it's all going to be right in the end.

Job didn't have that advantage. Job had no idea how it was going to end, if it was going to end, or why it had all gone so bad in the first place.

But I want to know. Now.

Living on a Need to Know Basis

It is the information age. I can find out pretty much anything through books, television, or the world wide web. Just Google it!

As a culture we value knowledge and pursue it. There are game shows where people compete to see who possesses greater knowledge. Remember Ken Jennings from *Jeopardy?* He seemed to know *everything.*

We also believe knowledge is power. If we know then we are in control.

In the beginning there was a tree and it was called the tree of the knowledge of good and evil. Of all that God created this was the one tree whose fruit man and woman could not eat.[7]

Then came the lie. Another voice in the garden. "You will not die if you eat this fruit," said the serpent, "Eat it and your eyes will be opened and you will be like God, knowing good and evil."

You will be like God.

What did the woman think that meant? Exactly like God? Equal to God? Did she understand that it might only be like God in *knowing?*

Fast forward and consider some shepherds outside of Bethlehem. An angel appeared to them, and his first words were: Fear not.[8]

Why were those the angel's first words? Because an angel appeared to the shepherds and suddenly, they *knew.* They knew that angels existed. They knew they were not alone. They knew what an angel sounded like, looked like, and they were afraid, sore afraid.

Faced with the *knowledge* of an angel, it is very clear we are not the biggest thing going. We are *not* like God, we are little and powerless and vulnerable, and we become afraid. Very afraid. Sore afraid.

We are made in God's image, but we don't have his perspective, his power, in fact you name it we ain't got it. So, here we are, *not* a lot like God, only now we *know.*

The woman saw that the tree was good for food, it was a delight to the eye, and it was desirable for gaining knowledge. She desired knowledge so she took it and ate and gave it to the man.

They ate the fruit and they recognized their nakedness and attempted to hide it and then hid themselves from God because they were afraid.

Afraid of what?

I think perhaps they were afraid of what they knew.

God told them not to eat from that tree, presumably because they didn't *need* to know good and evil. God walked with them every day in the garden. He was asking them to live on a need to know basis. But knowledge is power, and we want to *know.*

The thing is, they already knew all they needed to know.

They knew God.

"You should never open the door until everyone has their pants on. That's a rule to live by."

- Motherly wisdom being dispensed
in a bathroom stall in Atlanta's airport.

Potty Talk

I've come a long way. A really long way.

Our two youngest kids are 14 months apart. On purpose. Seriously.

I hated potty training. Hated it. And a big part of why I hated it was public restrooms.

Once you've potty trained your kid, if you are away from home, they have to use public restrooms. And what do small children who have just been potty trained do? They hang onto the toilet seat, let's face it, for dear life. I'm sure they are all afraid of falling in and being flushed away.

And what is the number one rule of public restrooms?
Do. Not. Touch. Anything.

Especially the toilet.

So, we're at a stalemate. Must potty train kids. They must not touch public toilets. What's a mom to do?

My first thought was wait until the kid went to kindergarten. Let them exchange information.

Kid to my kid, "Hey why do you make a rustling noise when you walk?"

My kid to other kids, "What's that room you go into? What do you do there?"

They exchange information, my kid comes home, "Hey Mom! Guess what I learned in school today?!"

Voila. No muss, no fuss.

I thought it was a good plan. Alas. Children must be potty trained to go to preschool.

I hated potty training.

My firstborn was actually on track to be trained very early, at 18 months or so. But then she fell and broke her leg.

And the number one rule about casts? Do not get it wet.

End of potty training.

When she was three and our son was just a newborn, we tried potty training again. And while we were in the midst of potty training our washing machine broke. This was in the days before Pull Ups, that's right, just regular cloth training pants that had to be washed. Consequently, I was hand washing training pants in the bathtub.

The only upside? It was February, and I thought, well, my great, great, great grandmother would have had to walk to a creek and break through the ice for water. I have hot water available indoors, so I've got that going for me.

But I told my husband, if we are going to have another child, we have to have it before our son is potty trained, because once he's trained, that's it. Window closed.

We both wanted another child. And we looked at each other and said, Yeah, let's have another kid. Yeah. Right now.

It took a month to get pregnant.

Fourteen months apart may not be the optimal space between siblings, I think most would find it a smidge on the close side, but it worked for us.

I don't remember potty training my son, but he is trained so it must have happened. There are probably notes in a journal somewhere, but at that point I had three kids, who remembers anything?

Our youngest was potty trained in three days. It was do or die. And my life was the one on the line. Remember, preschool requires kids to be potty trained, and preschool for my youngest two was starting in three days. And they were going to go to preschool. Both of them. So, time to learn how to use the potty. Right. Now.

And she did. Easiest thing in the world.

All my kids were around three when they were trained. Old enough to understand Mommy meant business when she said, Do. Not. Touch. The. Public. Toilet.

Sigh.

I don't know when or why my public toilet phobia began. My mom tells me I had it as a kid. We would be out at a restaurant and I would have to go potty. Mom says she would walk me to the restroom, and I would say, Uh, no, never mind. We would do this several times. And, I'm told, I never would actually go.

Now I have grandchildren. And the eldest is potty trained. He's three. And we like to have adventures when we're together, so we were at Greenfield Village, in Dearborn, Michigan. And in the middle of playing, my grandson turned to me and said, "Nama, I have to go potty."

Here it is. The dreaded public restroom scenario. I took his hand and said, "Let's do this."

The kid has great control and we made it to the restroom. And he went potty. Holding tightly to the toilet seat. And when he was finished, I lifted him off and washed his hands for dear life and we walked back to where his brother and grandpa were waiting. As though it were the most natural thing in the world.

Which, I suppose it is. But for me, that was a milestone. Apparently, I'm not alone because later that day I was in another restroom with a young mom who could've been me twenty-some years ago:

"I said, 'DON'T Touch the toilet! Stand still! What are you doing?! What did I tell you?! STOP TOUCHING THE TOILET!!'"

When I emerged from my stall, I saw a young girl being practically bathed in the sink by her very distraught mom. "There has got to be a better way to potty train," she lamented.

I was tempted to offer my Kindergarten Information Exchange Plan.

Once my kids were all potty trained, we decided we would like to be a dog family. But I told my husband, I'm not training a dog. The dog must come pre-trained. Training the kids was tough enough.

While reading the newspaper Larry found a classified ad (do I have to explain classifieds? Those were the Craig's List of our time printed in a newspaper that came to the house every day. Except they were shorter than Craig's list, like a telegram. Do I have to explain telegrams?)

My husband found a classified ad offering a seven-month-old golden lab, house trained, free to a good family.

Feeling we qualified as a good family we headed out to see this dog. Me and the kids in our minivan. Larry in a work truck. The dog was a bit of a distance from our home, and we took a freeway to get there in what turned out to be a pretty good snowstorm aspiring to be a blizzard.

My van had no heat, ergo no defroster, and the windshield wipers were beginning to get an icy crust built up on them that I would clear on the drivers' side by opening my window (while driving) and catching the wiper on its upswing and snapping it quickly hoping the ice would be knocked off. It was marginally effective.

We arrived at the home of the proffered dog. A very nice, clean home with a white couch and loveseat and two adorable little girls around my kids' ages. The little girls had been permitted the honor of naming the "free to a good home, house broken" dog, and they dubbed her Princess Jasmine Sparkles.

Well.

Princess Jasmine Sparkles was an active, friendly, big puppy, who we were told would not get on the furniture, would never take food from the kids, was housebroken and came with a crate, a blanket, 20 pounds of dog food and toys. All free, or $25 maybe, somewhere in there.

What a deal! Why would they offer such a great dog so cheap? Well, sadly, the father was allergic to her.

Aw, too bad.

My eldest two were very excited about the puppy, my youngest who was around three, was more interested in the little girls' toys. As she sat on the floor playing, she kept getting hit in the face with the dog's rather formidable tail.

Well, kids? What do you think? Should we take her home? Two votes yes, one no. You guessed it; the dissenting vote was from the one being whacked by the tail.

Majority rules.

Larry told me later that when he went to the basement to fold up the kennel and get all her paraphernalia that the kennel was adjacent to what was dad's desk and office workspace.

Larry concluded Dad was probably *not* allergic so much as Mrs. White Couch with the neat and clean house was not ready for a 70-pound furball to untidy everything.

So, we owned a dog. A large dog. Larry couldn't take her in the work truck, so I had to put this strange beast in the car with me and the three kids and head home.

Huh. The dog, being large, but also a puppy was very interested in getting under my feet while I was driving. She couldn't quite squeeze into the space with the gas and brake pedals, but she did succeed in pushing against all the buttons that moved my seat up and down, back and forth the whole way home in the snowstorm.

Now because we sort of imagined the dog as being our son's pet, Princess Jasmine Sparkles as a moniker just didn't really do it for any of us. We talked it out, and probably showing a little more respect than was necessary for the dog's psyche - see we didn't want to upset her by completely changing her name (do dogs know? *Really?*). We decided to simply shorten it to Sparkles.

Welcome to the family, Sparkles.

Some of Mrs. White Couch's assertions about the dog proved to be overstated and gave credence to Larry's theory that there were no "allergies" to overcome.

For instance, Sparkles had no trouble at all getting up on the furniture, in fact, she seemed to believe the couch was her bed and if we stayed up past 10pm she would come over and stare us down, It's getting late. Don't you people have somewhere to be? Like your own beds?

She showed no remorse over taking food from the kids, the counter, the bread drawer (which had to be moved if we wanted to eat the bread ourselves) and in her final years she managed to learn how to open the refrigerator.

And Sparkles chewed shoes and toys, giving us an opportunity to have a more inclusive doll community as many of them were now missing various limbs and were disabled.

She was a true retriever and every time Larry came home from work, she scrambled through the house searching for something to bring to him. We had learned to keep everything we didn't want chewed up off the floor, so all she ever found was a dirty sock. She proudly presented Larry with a dirty sock upon his every return.

But Mrs. White Couch told the truth when she said the dog was house broken, and to me this was The Most Important Thing.

Sparkles never had an accident in the house. Never. That was priceless.

And for a dog, *outside* of the house the whole world was her toilet.

This still presented a problem because the kids played in Sparkles' toilet, or what used to be our backyard. And inevitably they would step in dog poop.

Now there was no way on this earth a child was coming into my house with dog poop on their shoes.

Not. Going. To. Happen.

Shoe inspection took place at the door. "Let me see your feet, ok, ok, nope you stepped in poop, go out there and clean it off your shoe."

Trouble was, the kids were not good at cleaning the poop off their shoes.

The marked child would return, "I have cleaned my shoe."

"Let me see."

The dog poop was still there on the bottom of the shoe, only now it was wet.

"But Mom, I did the best I could."

"Maybe so," I would acknowledge, "but how much dog poop can be on the bottom of someone's shoe just before they walk across your pillow?"

"Ew! Mom! Gross! None! Yuck."

"Exactly. That is precisely how much dog poop you may bring into this house."

None.

My kids could never clean the dog poop off their shoes. Invariably I would have to go outside and do it for them before they were permitted in.

My kids aren't the only ones with a dirty shoe problem.

You see we have all been invited into God's house, to be with God. But we've got this dog poop on our shoes. Sometimes it's called sin. It's the bad, mean, selfish things we do, the thoughts we think. It's all the deeds, words, thoughts and motives that mark us as less than God. Less kind, less forgiving, less loving. Less than God, who is holy, righteous.

Call it what you will, we are not getting into God's house with it on our shoes.

But like my kids, we're never gonna be able to get it off by ourselves. Try though we might. We can't.

We simply cannot.

That's why Jesus came. He left his Father's house to let us know we were invited in, but we had this dog poop on us that was going to prevent us entry.

Good news: you're invited in. Bad news: your poopy shoes will prevent it.

Jesus didn't leave it there though. No, he came with *all* good news. He offers us his clean shoes for our poop covered ones. An exchange. Jesus' cleanness for our dirtiness.

Problem solved.

Welcome Home.

Only sometimes, sometimes, although I *want* the new shoes, I am reluctant to surrender the old. They're not *that* dirty, I rationalize. I like them. I will miss them.

But a choice must be made. To enter his house, to be with God I must choose to take his clean shoes. Or I keep the old and remain outside.

If we insist on keeping Hell (or even Earth) we shall not see Heaven:
if we accept Heaven, we shall not be able to retain
even the smallest and most intimate souvenirs of Hell.

C.S. Lewis[9]

Life is like a Toys R Us...some get to live in Barbie's Dream House,
and some of us live in a barrel of monkeys.

Elephants at the Circus

When I was a child my family went to the circus. The clearest
memory I have of that night, besides the really big wavy
balloons that we didn't get to buy, was the elephants.

More specifically, the elephant's poop.

It was huge. Like ottomans.

And there was a man who followed the elephants. His job was
to scoop their poop into a cart. Only one time he was being a
little too efficient and almost got pooped *on* as he was
scooping.

My dad and I laughed!

I have been diagnosed with depression. It seems to be
genetic, coming from both sides of my family tree. It took me
a long time to reach the place where I was diagnosed, and real
help came.

The journey began when my first child was born. Shortly
after her birth, we moved out of state and into my parents'
home so we could start a wedding photography business with
my dad.

Living as an adult, and as a parent, in my parents' home I was
able to observe things that perhaps had escaped me as a child
in their home.

There were some disturbing behaviors that my dad was

displaying, more disturbing because I recognized them in myself too. I looked at my daughter and thought, Nope, we are not passing this on, I have to figure out what this is.

It took nine years.

Meanwhile I was fighting through the darkness, the pain, the exhaustion that depression brings.

It was so exhausting. It didn't leave me with a lot of energy and sadly I misspent the energy I did have. I worked very hard to *prevent* anything that would require a lot of energy from happening. I was trying to control my environment.

That was not effective. And it resulted in crazy rules and crazy responses to my kids.

My son was very young when I realized he had keyed into my default response: No.

Whatever they asked, No.

So observant was he that he began asking questions differently:

"Why can't I .....?"

His logic must have been, her answer will be no, so let's skip to why.

My husband made a very helpful analogy for me. He said, "If your job is to scoop the elephant's poop, don't spend all your energy trying to keep them from pooping."

That's what I was doing.

So tired, so fearful that I wouldn't have enough in me to face whatever came, I worked doubly hard to try and control my whole world and force it to behave the way I thought was best.

Clearly, I had not evaluated the amount of energy spent in responding to life versus the amount of energy required to control life.

Controlling takes way more energy, mostly because it is a losing cause. I can't control the world.

I am, after all, not very much like God

"You broke the ship. You broke the bloody ship!"

Alex, *Galaxy Quest*[10]

It's the Whole World

When the first man and woman chose to trust a voice other than God's the repercussions were not limited to their relationship with God. No. It rippled out and impacted the whole world. The ground was cursed on their account.

In his letter to the Christ followers in Rome, Paul explains that all creation was subjected to frustration, not willingly. But it would be set free from its bondage to decay someday.

And it's waiting.

While we are waiting for everything to be set right, we have to live with the consequences.

We have to live in the brokenness that pervades our world.

It was a Saturday and shockingly I had nowhere to be. That does not mean I had nothing to do, just nowhere to be.

I started the day with my journal and my Bible. A good place to start. It was a good morning. And I knew what needed to be done: pay the bills, research some material for a prayer gathering, send some emails, go to the bank and deposit the paychecks that had been stacking up, take the dog to get her nails trimmed.

But when I came downstairs, it was apparent that a couple other things had jumped to the top of the list. Caramel, our cat for one. Caramel was 16 going on 17. And she was showing every day of it. She was a very old cat and that morning she appeared to be a cat that may not be getting too much older.

She was hanging out in the living room and wasn't really moving much. I had brought her food there- she still had a great appetite. But that morning I realized that Caramel was not making trips to the litter box in the basement. She hadn't gotten any further than the throw rug by the front door.

The first order of business became setting up a cozy little space for Caramel, complete with food, water, bed and litterbox. I used the puppy's kennel. But where to keep the puppy Mocha? I penned her in by putting up a gate by the basement landing.

Add that to the chore list. When I went to get the kennel, someone had peed in there too. Great. Now I had to wash down the kennel. And when I moved the kennel, I saw that my puppy had shed several smaller puppies worth of fur around the edges and I must vacuum.

When I pulled the vacuum out of the closet, I saw that it hadn't been emptied in a long time. Of course, I couldn't remember the last time I used it, so who knows. But the vacuum had to be emptied and the filter blown clean.

I took the dirty throw rug down to be washed. While vacuuming I saw that the floor really needed to be washed.

When I went to place Caramel into her new space, I discovered that she hadn't needed a litter box really, because most of the poop was stuck to her fur.

Time to bath the ancient old lady cat. Poor girl. Having set up the cat's new space, vacuumed and washed the floor, I looked around and realized the day was all but over and I hadn't even begun my original list.

We live a quiet life we tell ourselves. But Larry and I may be deluded.

A friend was coming to stay. So we decided to give the basement floor a serious cleaning. Spot cleanings after the cat's various digestive issues had not given us the "clean house smell" we were looking for.

We brought in the hose and a bottle of bleach. The result was a clean floor *and* potentially harmful gases which caused our eyes to burn and our throats to be sore.

After googling the possible harm we had caused ourselves, we went to bed. At midnight we were awakened by a phone call from our son. He was responding to some texts I had sent at a much more reasonable hour. But this is when his shift ends at work and it is always good to talk to him.

Since I was awake, I decided to make a trip down the hall. Mocha decided she needed to go out as well. I removed her collar in an attempt to stop the jingling that sometimes keeps us awake at night and I let her out.

Our backyard is dark and Mocha is brown, so I can't see her at night, but I heard some kind of commotion and opened the door to call her.

What I found instead, was a very scrawny, awkward looking skunk at the foot of my steps trapped between the house and the dog. A dog who desperately wanted to be back in the house.

I confess, my response was an expletive and an abrupt closing of the door. The skunk was confused and dashed back and forth across the bottom of the steps several times before heading for the driveway.

Mocha saw her chance and came for the door, which I opened, hoping to increase her speed as the skunk was not yet out of sight or range.

Brown fur shot past me into the house before I could assess any actual damage. She ran crazed upstairs and downstairs repeatedly, and with no collar I couldn't grab her. Larry and I eventually trapped her in the bathroom and saw that she was foaming profusely at the mouth. She had flicked this foam throughout the house before we trapped her.

I tried, in vain, to rinse her mouth in the bathtub. Finding no other part of her to be "hit" I gave up. Larry cleaned up the foamy spots on the floor.

My attempt to quarantine her and her smelly foamy mouth in the dining room failed. She and I ended up sleeping in a spare bedroom away from Larry who was not feeling well from the bleach and now skunk fumes.

We slept with all the windows open. The temperature that night? It was 43 degrees Fahrenheit.

And that is what a quiet night at the Schmidt House looks like.

Hearing my tale, a friend offered me a skunk trap to take care of my unwanted yard critter.

It was a "live" trap. What do you do with a live trapped skunk?

I couldn't kill it.

Because the "rest of the story" is that this same skunk, and I knew it was the same skunk because it was a small, goofy looking specimen, I encountered this same skunk in the daylight hours in my front yard when I was headed to work two weeks prior.

The skunk had a single serving yogurt container stuck on its head and it was wandering in circles in the street at the end of my driveway.

I have tried to help wildlife before...like the time a mother duck and her ducklings were walking down the tree lawn. Her last little duck was out of line, and off the curb in the street, which, as a mom, I saw as dangerous.

I stopped my car and got out to help the duckling back up onto the lawn and safety. Mama Duck didn't see it that way. She came after me. The final result was that all ducklings ended up on the lawn, objective achieved. But I looked more like the big, bad wolf, than the empathetic Good Samaritan Mom I was going for.

I knew better than to try and come to the aid of a skunk.

I was quite distressed, however, with his circumstances. I had watched him walk into the curb head/container first and jam it on tighter! I seriously asked God to release the skunk from the yogurt container and keep him from getting killed by a car while it was on his head.

When I came home from work there was no dead skunk in the street, and I rejoiced.

That's right. That's the rest of the story. I asked God to preserve the life of a skunk that lives to terrorize me in the night.

I had cleaned out my car.

Dropped a small bag of trash into my outdoor garbage can, and out of the corner of my eye spotted something furry moving in the bottom of the garbage can.

I gave the requisite scream and jumped back. Could not bring myself to look in again.

My neighbor bravely looked in and said, "It's a small possum."

Drat. Not a cat, a possum. Not only that, a baby possum.

Compassion overcame cowardice, it was very hot and there was no water in my garbage can, so I very cautiously tipped the garbage can down (with a rake) to free the poor little possum, who immediately made a break for home, which is under my shed in the back yard.

I have never cared for birds. Which some may find ironic. I

don't care for them, but I felt no malice to them.

That's changing. And I blame the birds.

First there was the seagull who helped himself to a sandwich right out of my hand on a beach in February. Now because I was *on* a beach in February, I didn't feel I had too much room to complain, though the startle factor was pretty intense.

These past two days it has been a trio of grackles. Nasty birds. Aggressive. Grackles are very defensive of their territory when nesting. For several days they have been dive bombing my dog and me in our backyard, and tonight in the front!

A group of grackles is referred to as a nuisance or plague. They certainly are.

I bought a fake hawk to scare them. It scares me much more than it scares them. It has fallen over twice today. I can't prove it, but I suspect it didn't fall by itself.

Gardening has become hazardous. When they dive, I end up screaming (forgive me ladies) like a girl! To the casual passerby I appear insane. Yelling and threatening birds. Trying to verbally intimidate them. Let's face it, that's all I've got.

They have the sky. I have words.

I'm losing.

I never felt malice for birds, but that's changed.

I have never cared for guns. And I have a great distaste for making things dead.

The grackles better hope that doesn't change too.

"What a day this has been, what a rare mood I'm in, why it's almost like being..."[11]

Dirty Jobs

Well, the song goes on to say, it's "almost like being in love." But that's not how I would finish the lyric today. Today it's "almost like being...Mike Rowe."

You know Mike Rowe? From the TV show *Dirty Jobs*? Love that guy. Really.

Wish he'd been here Thursday.

Thursday morning, I discovered that our basement had about an inch and a half of water on the floor. Not the first time, probably not the last. But never something I look forward to.

Called our reliable guy Chuck from Best Results Plumbing. Chuck came out and cleared my outside pipes, which were clogged with tree roots, string and other items that I have no *idea* how they got there. Truly.

And my brain wants to figure out mysteries like this (thank you, papa). It wants answers. That night I dreamt we had moved away from this house and then moved back and the people who lived here in between must have flushed these stupid things down the toilet. Not true, but apparently the only explanation my subconscious could come up with.

We have been here before. The water in my basement is not coming in from the outside, it is already here and finds it impossible to leave. So it stays. In the basement. Until Chuck comes and clears the way.

Once Chuck clears the way, my Handsome Prince then comes in with hose and bleach and makes it all better.

Only that didn't happen this time. This time there was no time. No spare time. My Handsome Prince had been working, a lot. And there was no time for him to make it all better. And frankly, it smelled. Not nice. And the house smelled. Not nice.

So I had to pony up and do it myself.

And I learned a few things about washing the basement floor. It is not a pleasant job to begin with, but my house, my precious house, where I have raised my family and lived and loved, this house makes the job harder. And here's why:

Top Five things that made this dirty job dirtier...

5. Not enough light

We have plenty of fluorescent light fixtures in the basement, but one by one they have stopped working. No, it's not the bulbs, we have replaced them. Consequently, anything done in the basement must be done with the light from the windows (therefore in the daytime) aided by one lone light bulb: 60 watts. The job must be done in the day. Handsome Prince works all day. Ergo, I must do the job, thus making it dirtier, for *me*.

4. The instinct that one should not be running a hose in the basement

Common sense says, do not pour water onto the basement floor. And yet, I must pour water onto the basement floor. This is not a bucket and mop job. This calls for more water. Lots more water.

I used a hose. Attached to the wash tub sink. A hose, a large broom, bleach, and a squeegee.

Initially, I was tentative about the hose, and very sparing with the water. I got over that. By the end I was enjoying hosing down the basement.

Though it did occur to me that perhaps the washer and dryer should not be running while I was pouring water underneath them. In fact, they should probably be unplugged.

Now kids, don't do this at home, I paused long enough to, successfully, unplug them both, and then resumed a very liberal application of water to the basement. I think I will wait until the floor and furnace duct vents are dry before plugging the washer and dryer back in.

If the ceiling is dry, the bottom of the washer and dryer should be too, right?

3. Clumping kitty litter

I have a cat. He requires a litter box. Clumping kitty litter is a wonderful innovation that makes litter clean up easier. Until my basement floods. Then clumping litter is a lot like grackles - a plague. I don't know how well I *haven't* swept the floor until I soak it and discover clumping kitty litter sludge. This must be swept up independently of the cleaning the floor. Don't want this sludge going down the drain, that will just cause the whole cycle to start over again.

2. Water soluble paint

You read that right. My basement floor was painted in water soluble red paint. Who does that? Who makes that?! I would like to know. What Einstein made it? What Genius bought it? And what Fool applied it to what has become *my* basement floor? Whenever the floor gets wet, the paint comes up and attaches itself to whatever is nearby: laundry, rugs, walls...

We painted over the red paint, with actual floor paint. In grey. Trouble is the grey paint is sticking to the red paint and the red paint isn't sticking to anything but my laundry. The result is a river of paint chips that must not be permitted to go down the drain, lest we begin the entire cycle again.

But preventing the paint chips from washing down the drain is not as hard as one would think, because of the number one thing that makes this dirty job dirtier...

1. Drains placed at the high points of the floor

I have two drains in my basement. Neither one is anywhere near the lowest point of the basement floor. In fact, the lowest part of the basement floor is underneath the stairs.

If there were a topographic map of my basement, you could name the two mountains Drain One and Drain Two.

The water must be encouraged, no, forced really, to go where no water wants to go: Up. Up to the drains.

This is best done with a broom. A squeegee is ok, but the floor resembles a ski hill of moguls and the squeegee is so long it does not make complete contact with the floor.

This gives the water an escape, a way to avoid doing what is unnatural.

So I used the broom mostly. And the hose. I hosed down the floor for a really long time. A really long time. When the basement stopped smelling bad, I knew it was time for the bleach.

Cool thing about bleach is that it makes little suds when scrubbed into the floor with a broom. After letting the bleach sit on the floor for a time, I picked up the hose again. Now, with the bleach suds I could see the way the water ran. Happily, it did seem to want to run away from the walls, so the floor by the walls must be slightly elevated.

As I've said, the big pond is under the stairs, with a slightly smaller pond just south of it, and separated by a nice mound of floor. The drain by the washer and dryer is useless. Completely useless.

The second drain, thankfully, is actually low enough to receive water. I knew I had enough water on the floor when I could make white caps with the broom.

And now my basement floor is clean. Wonderfully clean. The dirty job is done.

I believe I will reward myself with a trip to the library, where I can escape into someone else's world for a time. I love fiction, but I don't write it. No point. My life is stranger, messier, funnier and filled with more adventure than anything I could dream up.

And while I enjoy my sitcom, sometimes I like to turn the channel and enjoy someone else's for a time.

Old People

It's official. Larry and I have become Those Old People. You've seen them, the ones who are incredulous over something, like say, the price of a movie ticket...

We went to the movies tonight. And I knew, being Friday night, that we were going to pay full price (see, we already go for the discounts). But when the teenybopper cashier told me that two tickets for *The Lorax* at 5:20 would be $26, my jaw dropped.

What?! Did I miss a decade or two? I started looking around searching for more information to solve the mystery of this incredible price to view the adaptation of a Dr. Seuss book.

Ah, there's the trouble, the movie is in 3D.

3D?

I don't want 3D. 3D is **life**. I came to the movies to escape life. I am looking for 2D thank you. Something less intense than my life. Something with one less D.

But my debit card had already been swiped. So, as the teenybopper looked up at me through her bangs with disdain only achievable by one her age, I signed the receipt and took our tickets, and our 3D glasses.

We went into the theatre, after stopping at the restroom, found seats right in the center, put on our 3D glasses-over our regular glasses, settled in and...wait for it...

Fell asleep.

Sigh.

"I can see clearly now the rain is gone. I can see all obstacles in my way."[12]

Visual Acuity

I always seem to have a song running through my mind. Right now it is Johnny Nash's "I Can See Clearly Now."

While these are the lyrics in my brain, they are not the truth I am experiencing.

No, I *used* to see clearly. I used to have 20/15 vision. Which I thought was quite good. Better than, you know, the standard 20/20 we all hear about. Hindsight is 20/20. And that news show is 20/20.

As it turns out 20/20 is sort of the lower limit of normal, the bare minimum, if you will. The average visual acuity of healthy eyes is 20/16 to 20/12. So what I thought was great vision turns out to have just been average.

And I was so proud. I had 20/15. Mere mortals had 20/20, but *I* had 20/15.

Like this was something I accomplished myself. You too could have 20/15 vision if you just...what? Tried harder?

Well taking pride in something you had no hand in can backfire. Because I no longer have 20/15 vision. I don't know what the measurement is now, but I can tell you that I cannot read without my glasses, and I never had that problem before. I could read anything: near, far, small, large, computer, small print on pill bottles, I could see it all.

Now? I can't. So, having taken pride in my vision I wonder...is it my fault? How did I blow the good vision thing? Should I not have started using glasses? Did that do it?

No, the sad truth is that I can't see clearly anymore because of age.

I am aging. Getting old. Body parts are breaking down. Hair greying, skin wrinkling, you get the picture.

I don't see so well anymore. It is just a symptom.

But the underlying cause may not be what you think.

I don't see clearly anymore because I am aging. But is aging the cause or another symptom? Is there something deeper?

This is an important question. A proper diagnosis is vital to proper treatment. For an appropriate treatment we must discern if something is a symptom or the underlying cause.

It does no good to simply stop a symptom; say, pain. No one wants to be in pain, but if we don't get at the root cause, if we just take a pill to make the pain stop, we miss the whole disease or injury. And the pain will come back after the pill wears off, maybe with other symptoms, because the problem still exists.

My favorite example of proper diagnosis is an incident related in Chapter 2 of the *Gospel of Mark*. Jesus is teaching in a house. People find out he's there and come from great distances to hear him.

One group comes to do more than listen. Four fellows are carrying a friend to the house where Jesus is because their friend is paralyzed. They want Jesus to heal him. They want their friend to walk.

They get to the house, but can't even get near the door, the crowd is too big. In a true sitcom move, these determined friends go up on the roof. They then dig a hole in the roof and *lower their paralyzed friend into the house through the hole in the roof.*

Can you imagine? What was this guy feeling? He, being paralyzed, had no control over what they were doing. Was he glad? Embarrassed? Desperate to walk?

What kind of *mess* did this make? What was the homeowner thinking? Good thing the crowd was large, the owner probably couldn't get to the dudes on the roof.

The four buddies were likely feeling pretty good. Mission accomplished! They carried their friend, overcame the crowd and managed to lower him into the house *right in front of Jesus.*

Score!

Then, perhaps, they were peering in through the hole they made, waiting for the miracle, waiting to see the victory: their friend walking!

Jesus looks at the man and says, "My son, your sins are forgiven."

Yes! High Five! All right! ... wait, what?! What did he say? Sins? What sins?

Hey Jesus, we carried him here so you could make his legs work man!

They weren't the only ones confused by Jesus' statement. Some guys who spent their lives studying about God were more than a little bent out of shape by this statement. See, they knew only God could forgive sin. So...what? What was this guy Jesus claiming? Was he claiming to *be* God?

Jesus knew what they were thinking. And he addressed the God-guys, "Why are you thinking this? What is easier? To say, 'Your sins are forgiven' or to say, 'Get up and walk.' I want you to understand, I have authority to forgive sins."

Jesus looks at the paralytic and says, "Get up, take your mat and go home."

And he does.

The Great Physician makes a proper diagnosis: paralysis is a *symptom*. The cause? A world broken by sin. Original sin, my sin, your sin. Everything is busted. This is not how the world was created, this is a damaged version.

Jesus came to set it right.

The four friends just wanted their buddy to be able to walk. Jesus wanted him to be whole, be who he was meant to be, be reconciled to God. For that Jesus had to take out the underlying disease.

And, in case there was any doubt, he made the symptom go away too. A little visual aid.

Something to help us see clearly.

I still exhibit symptoms of the brokenness of this world. I

need my glasses to write this. My body is going to continue to break down until one day it gives out.

But...and this is a big but...the underlying cause of my aging eyes has been dealt with.

My sins are forgiven. Just like the dude with the four really good friends. Forgiveness was granted by Jesus. He had the authority to do it. It was a debt I owed. He paid it in full.

Driving, I saw a billboard which admonished us to stop distracted driving.

It had two photos on it; a woman and a man.

Who are they? I wondered and proceeded to read the captions. Ruth Johnson, Secretary of State of Michigan, and Mark Bernstein, lawyer.

I then looked back to the road to see the van in front of me had slowed down to make a right turn.

By quick application of brakes and swerving I narrowly escaped that horrible sound of two automobiles colliding and that horrible feeling of- What a mistake! THAT could've been avoided.

Stop distracted driving.

Yes. Indeed.

The Analogy of Great Price

I had been driving for 32 years. I fancied myself a good driver because in those 32 years I had never been pulled over by a police officer. Never pulled over, never ticketed.

My driving record was spotless. And I was proud of that. Who wouldn't be?

This fantasy ended one Monday morning. I was heading into work, enjoying a new CD, singing and in a very good mood. As I got closer to work, I saw flashing lights in my rear-view mirror. I pulled over. Turned off the CD. Rolled my window down and waited.

The officer approached and asked if I knew why he was pulling me over. I had no idea.

He told me I was speeding, going 15 mph above the posted limit. He asked for my driver's license, registration, proof of insurance. I found them all and handed them to him.

The officer asked me about my driving record, and I told him, it was spotless. This was the first time I had ever been pulled over. He walked back to his car.

When he returned, it was with a ticket. Graciously, he gave me a ticket that would not show up on my record with points, it would not trigger notice to my insurance company. It would, however, cost me a good deal of money.

And so it ended. My beautiful driving record that had no tickets was gone. Ruined.

But you know, just because I had never received a traffic ticket, didn't mean I had never deserved one. It meant I had never been caught speeding, or making a mistake, or breaking the law.

It didn't mean I was a perfect driver, it meant I *looked* like a perfect driver.

My life can be like that too. It can appear spotless, perfect, without blemish.

Sometimes I can look pretty good. That doesn't mean I am. Just because people don't see all my thoughts or actions, doesn't mean all my thoughts or actions are right. I can look good, but that doesn't mean I am good.

My "perfect" driving record, of which I was so proud, was a sham. I don't know how fast I was driving that Monday only because I was too busy singing to notice. But I know I have driven above the posted limit on other days.

I deserved that ticket, and I have deserved many more. How happy I am that I have not received as many tickets as I deserve. I couldn't afford it!

I can't afford to pay the penalty for my life record either.

Thank God I don't have to.

Maybe It's Maybelline?

Freshman year of college. I'm sick. Sick enough that I make an evening appointment at the health clinic.

While I'm waiting for my appointment time, I hang out in the main lobby of my dorm where a Mary Kay demonstration is taking place. Mary Kay is all about skin care, but they carry make-up as well. I'm not much for skin care and I don't wear make-up, but it's kind of like dress up: hard to resist playing.

I am easily talked into participating until I have to leave for my doctor appointment. I make it all the way through the face washing and right into the foundation and blush. Then I head out for the clinic.

When I get there, the doctor asks, "So, what can I do for you?"

I tell him I haven't been feeling well.

He looks at me funny, "You look healthy." I confess I have just come from a Mary Kay party.

The doctor is not amused. While he looks down my throat, he begins a loud rant about girls and make-up and nail polish and how they mask some health signs and make doctors' lives harder.

Then he tells me it looks like strep, does a culture and sends me off with an antibiotic prescription.

Guess my throat didn't look as good as my face.

I may have looked good on the outside, but that didn't

change the fact that I was a pretty sick puppy. I wasn't surprised though, I could feel it, I knew I was sick. Sometimes it is not that easy. Sometimes I look so good, I forget. I forget that looking good is different from being good.

In fact, sometimes I think it's all about appearances. What people see. But that doesn't go very deep. And just like my strep, my inner junk is there, and it isn't going to get better by itself. That's the whole point of the gospel, the good news. I'm not going to get better by myself. I need a physician.

So God sent one, the Great Physician, his son Jesus. Jesus, who took all my sickness, all my inner junk on himself and gave me his health.

Last night I was reading Oswald Chambers' My Utmost for His Highest....

> *What our Lord wants us to present to Him is not goodness, nor honesty, nor endeavor, but real solid sin; that is all He can take from us. And what does He give in exchange for our sin? Real solid righteousness. But we must relinquish all pretense of being anything, all claim of being worthy of God's consideration.* [13]

God wants me to let him look deep inside. He wants me to show him the junk, the sickness, the strep, the sin. No putting my best foot forward, this isn't about impressing God, that's all pretense.

So if I'm operating under the impression that I am looking good, I might want to stop and examine myself because...

Maybe it's Jesus, but maybe it's just Maybelline.

Lovable, Furry Old Grover

I do a pretty good impression of Grover from *Sesame Street*. This makes reading books with Grover in them even more enjoyable.

One of my kids' favorites was a book which Grover did not want us to finish.[14] He didn't want us to get to the end of the book. He was very adamant about us *not* turning pages.

Grover anticipated something bad at the end of the book and so just like us, he worked very hard to control his circumstances and keep as much distance as possible between himself and the end of the book. The entire book consisted of Grover attempting to stop us from going on.

You see, there was a *monster* at the end of that book.

I feel Grover's pain; I want to keep monsters as far away as possible too.

Monsters are scary. So I want to be very clear about defining them, identifying them and then doing everything in my power to protect myself from them.

Grover did everything he could to stop us from reaching the end of the book. He built brick walls, nailed pages together. But to no avail.

We reached the end of the book and the monster was.... Grover.

Phew. What a relief! Nothing to fear from Lovable, Furry, Old Grover.

The book ends well. Grover is a little embarrassed, but other than that, all is well.

My situation is a little bit different.

The monsters I try to protect myself from are scary and they inflict real pain.

But I have the same amount of success Grover did.

I cannot protect myself. I just can't. I cannot control the world or my circumstances. I am not all seeing, all knowing, or all powerful. Despite my best effort tragedy strikes.

And part of the problem is that, like Grover, I misidentify the monster. I think I can spot the monster, but if I am looking outward for the monster, I have missed the point.

You see, at the end of the day, *I* am the monster at the end of this book. In fact, every one of us is.

Apart from God, in this broken world, as broken people, every one of us is a monster and capable of inflicting great pain.

Want. What Do You Want?

Beauty pageant contestants know what *they* want...

Miss Utah? World Peace.

Miss Michigan? World Peace.

Miss New York? World Peace.

I hear them and I roll my eyes, yeah, yeah, yeah, good answer.

To want something is to desire it. I want a hot fudge sundae. I want to be on time. At one time I wanted to read the whole Bible.

I bought a One Year Chronological Bible. My New Year's resolution was to read through the entire thing in one year. I even thought I would like to read ahead so that I would complete the reading before the next Christmas.

I started out strong. I read every day. By the end of January, I was into the mid-February readings. And then it came to a dead halt. I don't remember why.

I had enlisted my Sunshine State Friend to be accountable with and at the end of February I went to visit her. Carol and I decided we would catch up with our reading together. We sat down, poolside, in the sunshine and began to read. The trouble was I couldn't go quickly. There were things to ponder and even to talk about together as we read.

But if I am going to read through the entire Bible, I don't have time to stop and think about it. At this pace I will never catch up! There's no time to stop and think or talk about it, I want to read the entire thing!

Want actually has two meanings. Commonly when want is used it means to desire something. I want world peace. I want to read the Bible. But the archaic meaning is "to lack something essential."

The Book of Joel begins by describing a devastation of the land of Israel by locust. What the gnawing locust left, the swarming locust ate, what the swarming locust left the creeping locust had eaten, what they left the stripping locust had eaten.

After that there was nothing left. There was nothing for the animals to eat. Nothing to offer on the altar to God. The people were starving. Drunks were sober, there was no wine. There was *nothing.*

The people of Israel wanted food. They both desired it and lacked it. Because they lacked it, they desired it all the more. It is, after all, essential for survival. It's probable that they were frantic with searching for food. How do we get food?!

God offers a solution.

Declare a holy fast.

Seriously? *Fast?* Give up eating?! No problem. We've got that pretty well covered. Thanks.

There is **no** food - not like when your teenager says, "there's nothing to eat." This is a famine and there is nothing to eat.

NOTHING.

And when the people cry out to God, He directs them to declare a holy fast.

But God's not joking. He knows they desire food. He also knows what they lack.

You see in a famine you are looking for food, but when you fast you are looking at God.

When Jesus was walking the earth God the Father spoke audibly twice. Can you imagine? What was that like? I wonder what impact that had on the people who could hear it. God spoke out loud twice.

The first time was when Jesus went to John to be baptized. God said, "This is my Son, whom I love; with him I am well pleased."[15]

At the transfiguration God said pretty much the same thing. John, James and Peter are on the mountain with Jesus and God speaks, "This is my Son, whom I love; with him I am well pleased. Listen to him!"[16]

Listen to him.

Jesus was visiting a home and one of the hosts, Mary, was sitting at his feet listening to him teach. Her sister, Martha, however, was very busy. Too busy to sit down. Martha was scrambling trying to prepare enough food for Jesus and his entourage. Martha was all bent out of shape about everything that needed to be done, and she appealed to Jesus, Make my sister help me. Don't you care?[17]

But Jesus told Martha that her sister Mary made a better choice. Mary chose to sit at Jesus' feet and listen to him.

48

Jesus wasn't going to talk forever. It's not like his life was one long monologue. He would eventually stop teaching and *then* they could get a meal together. Martha had a choice: stay all hot and bothered or stop and listen, then work.

My firstborn was just over a year old and I was pregnant. I decided to get on the ball, and I wrote a bunch of letters, maybe as many as eight, to friends from out of state announcing the expectation of our second child.

My daughter and I ran some errands, mailed the letters, worked a bit at my parents' house. When I returned home, I noticed that I was bleeding.

Being the sensible person that I am, I immediately laid down on the floor with my feet in the air and called my OB.

It was February 1988 and I was twelve weeks into my second pregnancy. I went to the hospital. When I left I was no longer pregnant. I left the hospital wanting my unborn child.

Arriving home, I wanted my 16-month-old daughter. I sat on the floor wanting to take her in my arms and hug her and love her. I wanted to be with her. And she wanted...

Scissors.

She had spied some scissors and was asking for them, getting frustrated with my "no" answer, and she began to cry and fuss and reach for them.

As I sat on the floor I thought, Daughter, I know you want the scissors, but here I am, come be with me.

God showed me in that moment that in the same way my daughter was looking beyond me and the love I was offering, to cry after scissors, I was looking past him for what I wanted.

If the Bible could be distilled down to its most basic message you might be able to say it with three words: Look at God.

That is hard to do. Looking at God is what stopped when sin entered the picture. The woman and man were looking to hide after not trusting God. They didn't want to see God and they didn't want God to see them. They stopped walking together.

When they stopped desiring God all they lacked was God.

God invites me back to himself. He invites me to throw myself upon his lap like a child and pour out the desires of my heart. The deepest thoughts, the things that grieve me. He invites me to tell him what I want, what I desire. But I shouldn't jump up from his lap when my emotion is spent. I shouldn't leave after I have poured out my heart.

I am invited to choose the better thing.

Stay in God's lap and let him teach me what I lack, let him teach me to want him, to trust him.

God says, All you are wanting is me.

Want me.

Talk to Me

I have three children, and as anyone who has more than one child knows, they are as different as night and day and .... outer space!

My firstborn talks. A lot. With energy and enthusiasm.

My middle child is quiet. Watchful. Observant.

My youngest is a spark plug, but finding words can be a challenge, this one would rather dance it out than speak.

And I love to talk to them all. In their own way. I enjoy sitting in silence waiting for my middle child to share. I am energized by the work it takes sometimes to verbally reach understanding with my youngest. And I cherish the rushing river of words from my firstborn.

I do not look for a spokesperson. If one of them has something to say, to share, to ask, I want them to come directly to me and tell me, themselves. To have a spokesperson is to put distance between me and them.

Sometimes a third-party is necessary. I watched a few episodes of a reality TV show in which Marlee Matlin participated. Marlee is deaf, and so she had an interpreter with her. It sped up communication and helped with accuracy. But it also distanced her from her fellow participants.

I noticed that several of them didn't look at Marlee when they were talking to her. They looked at her interpreter.

I wonder how she felt about that. Words are only part of the connection. Focus, eye contact, body language, all play a part in communication and connection. I wonder if she ever wanted to shout, Look at me, talk to *me*!

I think that can happen when I pray. I look at the wrong person. I might look at my pastor, or a friend. I want them to pray instead of me. Do I think they do it *better*? As though it was a performance?

Prayer. Something has been lost with that word. It's become something we "do." Something that "works" or "doesn't work."

But prayer is simply talking. Talking to God. Myself. In my own way. And it's okay.

God is not deaf. He does not require an interpreter. He will not misunderstand me, because he understands me better than I understand myself or anything else really.

I believe he wants to talk to me. Wants me to talk to him. I think the evidence for that is pretty clear.

And when I talk to him, I ought to look at *him*. Talk to him, not *at* him. There's a difference.

I don't need to rely on others to do all the talking. I have things in my heart; things to say, to ask, to confess. He wants to hear those things from me. And from you.

So let's go for it. Stutter it out, shout it out, sing it out, use the King's English or use slang. Act it out. Take our time. Sit in silence. Or verbally throw up all over him. This is what he wants.

Why am I so certain? Because God loved us enough to send

his son so everyone who trusts his son has eternal life. And *this* is eternal life: To know God and Jesus Christ, whom God sent.[18]

He sent his son so we could know him. The best way to begin to get to know him is by talking to him.

CHOOSING COMEDY

Seasons

CHOOSING COMEDY

I'm in a hurry to get things done,
I rush and rush until life's no fun.
All I've really got to do is live and die,
but I'm in a hurry and don't know why.

Alabama[19]

Rhythm

There used to be a rhythm to the seasons and holidays. A flow, and a pace that was pleasant and varied. Rather like waves on the lake, or ripples in a pond, gently rolling, up and down...

I miss that.

It seems to me that we now brace ourselves *against* holidays. Before the Halloween candy can go on sale, the Christmas decorations are up, and we brace ourselves, "**No,** not yet."

I was in the grocery store, it was December 21, and someone had put up an Easter display. I am not making this up. The woman behind me in line couldn't believe it either, I could feel her tensing against that rush to the next thing. Bracing herself against the decorations that came too soon.

I suppose this is what comes of a consumer economy. Although all economies are based largely on consumption of goods, in America we already have all that we need and so our economy must be based on consuming things we do not need, and lots of them.

Holidays help that consumption by offering something different like M&Ms of varying colors: pink in February, green in March, Red and Green at Christmas.

But we must not allow for a lapse.

Personally, I try to stay out of stores between Halloween and Thanksgiving. If I must go to Target, I refuse to look up and acknowledge the offending decorations that are displayed weeks before the actual month of their holiday's celebration.

I brace myself by avoiding radio stations that promise to kill any enjoyment of seasonal music by playing it over and over and over until it is as unwelcome as leftover meatloaf served too many nights in a row.

Once Thanksgiving comes, I am prepared to welcome the next season. I desire to walk leisurely toward its celebration. But every day brings increased pressure to hasten, hurry, get ready. Though I want to walk slowly, I get caught up in the hustle and bustle, rush and rush, until the day finally comes and then.....

It's over. Abruptly. Done. Now.

And the next holiday is thrust at me like a forkful of food, before I have had a chance to savor, let alone chew and swallow, the current mouthful.

This frantic pace, like a piece of music played much too fast, is unpleasant. I enjoy an upbeat song. But when the tempo increases and increases and increases unrelentingly, at some point it ceases to be music and is simply noise.

I need silence. I need stillness. I need time to reflect, to think, to pray.

We tend to drive fast in Detroit. One of our freeways, I 696, is jokingly referred to as the Autobahn, that German highway with no federally enforced speed limit. On *any* given Detroit freeway, you get the impression that the speed limit is more like the Pirate Code, not a law really, merely a suggestion.

Which is fine as long as you don't mind the occasional police officer giving you a ticket for failing to take the suggestion seriously.

Speed is subject to the laws of physics and the principle that comes into play here is this: the faster an object travels the longer it will take to stop.

I don't think I grasp this concept very well.

The faster I go, the longer it takes me to stop.

I can go pretty fast.

But life is better when I am not hurried. The best conversations take place while sitting with a close friend over, not a cup, but a pot of tea or coffee. Relaxing in front of a fireplace, with nowhere to go. Walking slowly on the beach, no purpose, just strolling along.

I hunger for these kinds of moments. These times of conversation, not just with friends and family, but also with God.

So how do I create a rhythm that gives me space for silence, stillness?

How slow do I have to go?

That is the answer I am searching for.

Zoom, zoom.

Over the river, and through the wood,
To Grandmother's house we go...

Thanksgiving dinner for the past few years has featured beef as the main course. Why? Oh...now I remember....

Giving Thanks

Yes, yes, I am thankful, for many things. At the moment I am thankful that I don't have to actually kill my meals and prepare them any more than necessary.

My favorite part of Thanksgiving dinner? The stuffing (mom and dad have the best recipe!)

Least favorite? Wrestling a large dead bird. And that's where we are right now.

Aren't they supposed to come pre-plucked? Isn't someone paid to do that? Isn't the job description to rip ALL the feathers off this bird before it is packaged?

Well, whoever worked on my bird should not be getting a Christmas bonus. Pulling partial quills out of my bird's butt was not on my morning agenda.

And whose idea was it to stuff the turkey's neck up its behind? Hmmm? No dignity at all.

I'm worried about what I will find. The folks who prepped my turkey look like slackers...if there is a head on this bird's neck when I free it then dinner is over, I will see you at Red Lobster!

You are the baby of the house,
You're not as quiet as a mouse,
You make some noise,
So do your toys

But when the baby of the house
Is now as quiet as a mouse
Don't hear a peep
Cuz he's asleep

The Day Before Christmas

'Twas the day before Christmas and all through the house, not a creature was stirring...

My grandson is asleep. And my youngest is asleep. My oldest is out doing some last-minute shopping with her husband. My husband is working, making sure everyone gets the auto parts they need, as long as they come in before noon. And my middle child is probably grilling up steaks for folks who have decided lunch at Outback Steakhouse is just the thing on Christmas Eve.

There is so much about this season that I enjoy; the cookies, the anticipation, the music, the lights. I have many Christmas trees, a forest really, with white lights, all around the house. I like to sit in the dark with all the trees lit. And the gifts. I really enjoy giving gifts.

All my presents are bought, wrapped and waiting. Some are known, some are surprises.

I like to give gifts that are surprises. Others in my family prefer to work from a list. Sometimes I focus on desires and dreams. Other times I try to meet needs with my gifts.

My youngest prefers gifts in bags or special boxes that can be reused. For one of my friends wrapping gifts is part of the beauty of the season, her gifts all come with elaborate bows. Myself, I want to disguise a gift, conceal the gift's identity.

Gift giving can be extravagant or sensible. I never mean to go overboard. I intend to be sensible. But I often end up going overboard once I start.

When I harken back to what started this season of celebration, I see where many of the traditions began.

A father decided to give a gift...he didn't keep his gift a secret, and yet it was a huge surprise.

It was a gift that satisfied desires and dreams, and yet it was a gift that was desperately needed.

The gift was wrapped in cloth and it was well disguised.

And this gift was the very definition of extravagant. A gift that contained all the love a father could give.

And when it was given there was light, a very special light. And there was music, loud, heavenly music.

A messenger announced the gift: I bring you news of great joy for **everyone**! For a baby has been born, a Savior who is Christ the Lord. You will find him wrapped in cloths, lying in a manger.[20]

The King of the universe disguised as a baby.

He is given because his father knows what we desire and what we need.

And the cost of this gift is so great, so extravagant that there should be no doubt at all that the father has given this gift because he loves us so very much.

Someone's Knocking at the Door

After eight years of marriage, and eight moves, we bought a house. We couldn't really buy a "starter" house, because with two kids and a third on the way we weren't exactly a "starter" family.

We moved in in late October. Then we moved back out, so Larry could refinish the floors. It was 1990, but the carpet, an orange shag, was from the 70s, and it had to go. We moved back in time for the holidays and had been living in the house about five weeks when we observed our first New Year's Eve.

Two children were nestled all snug in their beds, the third was nestled all snug in me, just a few weeks till her debut. As midnight approached Larry was sleeping on the couch and I was watching a movie...when suddenly there came a knock at the door:

Bang! Bang! Bang!

"Larry! Wake up, someone's at the door!"

Larry jumped off the couch and ran straight to the window furthest from the front door.

"Lar, the door is over there," I pointed impatiently, irritated that he should be asleep with someone at our door in the middle of the night.

He staggered back to the middle of the living room. Then he asked, "What time is it?"

"Midnight," I answered.

He visibly relaxed and said, "Don't worry about it, it's just the Fourth of July."

I was not reassured.

"LARRY, someone was knocking at the door, WAKE UP."

"No one is at the door," he explained patiently. "What you hear is semi-automatic gun fire."

I was even less reassured. "Excuse me?"

"It's midnight, New Year, people are shooting their guns in celebration."

Well, of course, silly me.

Larry went back to the couch and I hoisted my eight-month pregnant self up the stairs to check on my babies. Specifically, to be sure no bullets had come falling through the roof. None had.

Over the years we have devised some customs to survive the ringing in of the new year by amateur soldiers and their very real weapons.

As other families watch the ball descend in Times Square, my children are "assuming the position" off the furniture and onto the floor. To be below the windows. Just in case.

We try not to go out on New Year's Eve. It can take a while for our neighbors to exhaust their interest and ammunition and we don't want to be driving back into the neighborhood before they do.

For that same reason we rarely invite anyone over on New Year's Eve. An invitation must carry the caveat of either a planned early departure, say before 11:45pm, or a commitment to stick around till 1am. We have entertained a few friends over the years, no one more than once.

I have a very serious attitude toward guns. I wouldn't say I have a respect for guns, more like an extreme fear. I was very intentional and scary when it came to teaching my children about them. *Always* assume they are loaded. *Never* point one at anything you don't intend to kill. If your friend or cousin should pull out a gun at their home *run immediately* to the nearest adult.

Just about a year ago I actually handled a gun. At a firing range. Shot it and everything.

You would think with my unhealthy fear I would have been a model of safety.

Not so much.

The trigger wasn't working and so I turned the gun to look at it and when I did, I pulled the trigger and it went off, cutting across the shooting range, rather than toward the targets.

And I was sober.

Consequently, I don't trust my "celebrating" neighbors one bit. Not even a little.

So we observe a quiet New Year's Eve at home.

On our twenty-first New Year's Eve in our home I was reading on the loveseat. Larry was sleeping on the couch. I had just pulled out my phone to text "Happy New Year" to my folks and kids, when...

Bang! Bang! Bang!

Our dog barked and rushed to the window. Larry startled awake and said, "Someone's knocking at the door!"

"No dear," I calmly replied. "It's just midnight. Happy New Year."

Knowing God a Little Better

In the beginning...Eve is the first woman. Eve was deceived, she and Adam disobeyed God. Sin and death were the result.

But God knew and had a plan, and part of the amazing goodness of this plan was that he allowed our salvation, our hope, our redemption to come into the world the same way sin and death came into the world: through a woman.

Having a baby boy at Christmas was a remarkable opportunity to wonder about Mary and her privilege, her honor, her responsibility, her journey.

Through my children God has taught me about myself as his child and given me the slightest glimpse of his perspective on me.

Every frustration I have experienced with my children has been turned around and I have looked to God and said, Is this what I do to you? Is this how I look and sound to you?

Holding my children when they were sick, I took joy in being their safe place and tenderly nursing them in their sickness.

After having more than one child I learned that love does not have limits, there is not a well that runs dry, there are no favorites. To have more children is simply to love more.

A mother's love is something marveled at the world over. But God says his love is more.

> Can a mother forget the baby at her breast
> and have no compassion on the child she has borne?
> Though she may forget, I will not forget you![21]

I may be one among the billions of people God has designed, but he tells me he knows me. He knows the number of hairs on my head.[22] He collects my tears.[23] He knows me completely; he is the one who designed me.[24]

In recognizing that my children don't see things the way I see them I have learned the limits of my own perspective.

> *"For my thoughts are not your thoughts,*
> *neither are your ways my ways,"*
> *declares the Lord.*
>
> *As the heavens are higher than the earth,*
> *so are my ways higher than your ways*
> *and my thoughts than your thoughts.*[25]

"Why can she do that and I can't?" one would cry. "It's not fair!" declared another. "You don't love me!"

I knew better. I knew what I desired most for them. And sometimes I knew how to guide them there.

But there have also been the very painful lessons, the lessons that showed me that no matter how much I loved my children, no matter what I knew, or what I did, I am not that much like God.

I fail, he does not. I falter, he is steadfast. My love is imperfect, his is perfect.

It Takes a Village

My phone started going off early, bringing Happy Mother's Day wishes.

The first was a number neither my phone nor I recognized. "Uh oh," said Larry thinking it was misdialed, "Someone's mom isn't getting her message."

The second was from a friend, he and his wife mentored Larry and I in our early days of marriage.

The third was from my "oldest" friend, not that she is chronologically older than all my other friends but having met in high school our friendship spans the most years. This is the friend that "knew me when." One of the few who knows all my history, my family of origin. The closest thing I have to a sister.

And it started me thinking. I wouldn't be the mother I am without these two and many, many more.

I'm so grateful for my mom, whom I mother so very much like. She set the example as my mom, and walked me through the earliest, scariest days, of my motherhood. Those days before I understood how fragile my children were *not*, either physically or mentally.

Then there was Larry's mom who, in raising him, formed the other piece of the foundation that would become the culture of our family. She raised me a good, good man. I am so glad to be the mother of his children.

I had a friend who spent full days with me during the dark days of my undiagnosed depression and made those days so very much brighter by her presence, her friendship, her wisdom as a teacher, her love for me and the kids.

My "oldest" friends from high school. We were moms alongside one another, tossing our kids together in front of Beatrix Potter, or in the "toy rooms" of our homes, while we took a breath with someone safe and encouraged each other along the way. We made the entire journey together, and it continues...

There were older women who were just far enough ahead of me to leave me a true path to follow.

And the Five Points moms, we were a village within the village, an extended family, a neighborhood like everyone should have. They were each "mom" to my kids in very special ways, and dear friends to me.

Later came women who entered my village as our mothering transitioned, as our children reached adulthood and we became more coach and peer and even - grandmas.

There was a man in my village, someone I never met, but he shaped my mothering in significant ways...Mr. Rogers.

There were women who became my sisters by marriage.

It takes a village to raise children. I'm so grateful for my village.

Once Upon A Time

My old flip phone was giving me trouble. At the time my three kids were in their 20s and we didn't so much talk on the phone as we texted. The buttons on my old phone were only working intermittently, which made for some unique messages since I didn't always get the letters I was trying for.

So I "upgraded." New phone, for free, as long as I promise my allegiance to my phone company for two more years. Why not?

But changing phones is a bit of a chore these days. I don't know anyone's phone number anymore. I dial by name. And my "contacts" are quite numerous. So those have to be transferred to the new phone.

And then there are the messages. And calendar. And photos.

This is not going from a chunky rotary dial phone to a sleek princess push button phone. That just required unplugging the old and plugging in the new. This transition is a technological event.

Especially the photos. I hate the idea of losing photos. Sure, it may just be a fraction of a second in time, but it captured someone I love, and I don't want to give it up. Portrait studios loved to see me coming.

I spent the morning texting photos from my old phone to my email address so I could download them on my computer.

Processing all those photos reminded me of a joke my husband and I used to make when we would attend social events without our kids. When asked about our children we would proudly produce a photo or two of our smiling cherubs.

If pressed as to why they weren't with us we would answer, "Because they are so well-behaved in photographs."

And that is the beauty of photographs. And the temptation.

I am sorely tempted to sit at my computer all day and just look at pictures. Pictures of smiling faces. Younger, fresher faces. We are all so still in the photos. It's all very contained. All very controlled. Tidy.

It may have been hot the day the photo was taken, but I can't feel it today.

Who knows what all was swirling around emotionally at the time the picture was snapped? All I see is the fraction of a second recorded. And it's very doable. I can live there.

Two of the photos from my old phone were of something I wrote at a wedding. It was the wedding of one of the boys who grew up with my kids on our street. One of the Five Points Family as we call ourselves. It was nostalgic and sweet...

> *Once upon a time there was a special place in Redford...where little rascals drove a Blur, and played for the Stanley Cup, and grew to be strong in the Force by kicking the can. Autumn was festive, in the spring eggs were hunted, and the night sky was bright in July. Grass would not grow there but children thrived and so did love, and the harvest yielded memories galore.*

Auld Lang Syne. Days gone by.

CHOOSING COMEDY

Moments passed yet captured. Memories.

I am tempted to live there.

But I won't. I will push myself away from all the photos of
yesterday (now that I have saved them). And I will boldly go
where I have not yet gone...

Into the next moment. I will dare to live in the unknown of
the next moment. I will live in its messiness and I will take
the camera in my phone and capture some fractions of those
future moments.

And I will wait for the day when these as yet uncaptured
moments are the moments of days gone by. When they will
seem safe and comfortable and nostalgic.

And gazing at them I will think, look how well-behaved we all
are.

Motherhood: the state of being perpetually wet.

How to Raise *My* Kids

Raising kids is tough. One reason is that there are no timeouts once you begin this game. No chance to gather your wits about you, no way to catch a breath. Once you have a child you are on, in the game, 24/7, set, go!

I don't have it all together now. I had it less together when my kids were young. But when kids are small, we are big and they think we know everything. Until they don't.

One evening I was standing at the stove making dinner. My eldest, who was beyond the "mommy and daddy know everything" stage and firmly in the "Who do you think you are to correct me?" stage, had done something I felt needed correcting.

Being the good mother that I am, I corrected her.

She immediately shot back, "Yeah, well you do thus and such!"

It was true.

I responded, "Yes, I do thus and such, and I am wrong. But if you want to wait until I am perfect before I can parent you, you will never have a mother."

On another occasion I was trying to explain something to my youngest. She wasn't challenging my authority or knowledge, she was defending herself and her perspective by responding, "I'm not stupid you know."

I did know. She is not stupid.

How to explain to a young person that correcting them was not an indictment against their abilities?

I told her, You are not stupid. You are just younger than I am. I have seen more than you have seen and therefore I have a better perspective.

It's like the Eiffel Tower. When you are young you are at the bottom of the Eiffel Tower, when you look out you see a bush. You see the bush, but that is all you see.

As you age you progress up the tower and the higher you get the more you can see.

Being older, I am higher up on the tower. I am not smarter than you, however, I do see more than you can see right now.

This analogy worked for her, but perhaps she applied it too liberally. Perhaps she thought I could see everything.

I didn't help this misconception when she called me from college, lost in a grocery store.

"Mom, I can't find the peanut butter."

She was eight hours away. She wasn't in danger, but she was my baby and she wanted peanut butter. I wracked my brain, "Well, I'm not there, but in our store it is in Aisle 8, try that."

I was correct.

The myth grew.

Unbeknownst to me from that day on I was her "Google." Don't know something? Ask mom. The texts came in at all times of the day and night. The questions seemed so random. I had no idea I was her go-to for knowledge. Frankly, I was Googling half the things she asked.

Home on a break from college we went shopping to get her some shoes.

Shoe shopping is different now, from when I was young. Back in the day there were actual shoe stores. That's all they sold: shoes. And when you went into the shoe store you sat down on a chair and a salesperson came over to help you.

The very first thing the salesperson did was to measure your feet. You took off your shoe and placed your heel in the curved metal of this flat contraption on the floor and stood up and the salesperson moved a sliding piece to the tip of your big toe and another sliding piece to the side of your foot and you stepped off. Then they repeated the process with your other foot.

Having determined your size they asked you what you were looking for, and if you had seen something you liked on display they would go in the back and bring out your size, and a couple of other choices in your size in the same shoe genre.

When you tried the shoes on, the salesperson pushed their thumb on the top of your big toe and asked how it fit.

That's not how it works anymore, at least not in my world. In my world we now walk around shelves of boxes of shoes looking at the shoe displayed on the top. If we find something we like, we begin searching the boxes for that shoe in our size. If we are lucky and find it, we try the shoe on.

My daughter tried on a pair of shoes. I asked, "How do they fit?"

"Ok."

I said, "Let me see." And I pushed the toe to see if there was a smidge of room.

She, in a question that would shatter her life, asked, "Why do you do that?"

And I, answering honestly without understanding the ramifications said, "I don't really know."

My daughter's head exploded. "You don't KNOW?!?!"

"Uh, no. I think I do it because I am seeing if there is enough room for your toe, or maybe I do it to see if there is room to grow. I don't really know."

"I thought you knew everything! My whole childhood was a lie!"

Oops.

The myth was shattered, by my own hand. She was devastated.

And in a way so was I.

I liked being the answer person. The one who could figure out where the peanut butter was from 453 miles away.

It can be tempting. Tempting to think of myself as being in a position of strength, being powerful enough to accomplish something, for others or even for God.

Take Moses.[26] His parents defied the law and did not allow their newborn son to be killed. Then they placed him in a basket in a river and he floated down to Pharaoh's daughter and was adopted. Saved. Grows up in Pharaoh's house. A place of significant power.

Moses knows who he is. He is a Hebrew. And he sees that the Hebrews are enslaved and in need of rescue.

From my (very limited) perspective, I might reason that Moses was saved in the river, to be placed *inside* Pharaoh's house, where all the power was, so that God could use him from that position of strength to deliver God's people.

But that's not how it worked. God actually used Moses from *outside* Pharaoh's house.

Moses actually left Pharaoh's house in fear and desperation. He tried to stand up for the Hebrews in his own power, by killing a man who beat a Hebrew. But that didn't gain the confidence of the Hebrews and put him in a bad place with the Egyptians.

After giving him a long time-out God sent Moses back to Pharaoh. God directed Moses to defy the power of the land and threaten him in ways only God could see through. How's that for taking a risk? There was no way Moses was going to be able to protect himself if it went bad. And by going bad I mean if God didn't do what he said he'd do.

Moses was out on a limb. Rather than working from a false position of strength, Moses was fully dependent on God to come through and do what Moses himself never could.

James, the brother of Jesus, warns against pride, vanity, and boasting in the Book of James, his letter to followers of Jesus.

"Come now, you who say, 'Today or tomorrow we will go to such and such a city, spend a year there, buy and sell, and make a profit.' Whereas you do not know what will happen tomorrow. For what is your life? It is even a vapor that appears for a little time and then vanishes away. Instead you ought to say, 'If the Lord wills, we shall live and do this or that.'"[27]

James is warning his readers not to imagine they have significant power or strength. He tries to put it in perspective with the reminder that everything is dependent on God.

I always forget that important middle part. I read it: If the Lord wills, we will do this or that.

But no, it is...

If the Lord wills, we shall *live*.

If the Lord wills. We shall live.

It's a word of caution. I can get carried away with my very limited perspective and I forget that what I see is not all there is, in fact, what I see is not most of what there is.

What I see is a bush.

Pomp and Circumstance

The woman who hosts an NPR advice feature called "Ask Amy" was herself seeking advice. She was scheduled to speak at a high school commencement. What should she say?

It was a diverse graduating class. And it was a high school. Some would go into the military, some would go on to college, some would enter the work force. What could she say that would be relevant to ALL of them?

As I mulled it over I began to have some ideas, so....

To the Graduating Class

The birth of a child is a celebration. It is a miracle. A new person, a fresh person, full of promise and possibilities. Holding a newborn and gazing at their unique face one wonders, who are you? What will you become?

A lot of growing and learning must take place, but eventually that brand-new person finds them self on a threshold, as you are today.

Commencement is a threshold moment, you will walk forward and begin to answer those questions: Who am I? What am I becoming?

As we are paused in this doorway, I would like to address a lie you have likely been told. It is actually two lies. You have been told something, but you may have heard something else. What you heard and what was said are both lies.

You may have been told *You can be anything you want to be.*

What you likely heard was *You can do everything you want to do.* It's not true. You can't.

You cannot *do everything*, you cannot *have everything*, you cannot *be everything*. You can't.

You must make choices.

This is an often-misunderstood principle of economics: cost. What does something cost?

Let's make it simple...a CD costs $15. Two tickets to a movie cost $15. A shirt costs $15.

I buy the CD. I paid $15.

But that is not the final cost. What has to be figured in is what it cost in opportunities not chosen. Items not purchased. I bought a CD, it cost me $15 AND it cost me two movie tickets and a shirt.

Why? Because once the $15 is spent I cannot spend it again.

Once a day is spent, it is spent. You do not have time to do everything. You do not have the energy to do everything.

You may do many things. You cannot do everything.

But that only addresses the lie you heard. We have not yet addressed the lie that was stated.

You can be anything you want when you grow up.

No, you can't. You really can't.

It sounds encouraging to say to a second grader- You can be anything you want to be.

But it's not true.

A friend sent me a meme that illustrated this perfectly. A black and tan Dachshund was pictured standing on stilts. The caption read, "They said I could be anything I want. I want to be a Doberman."

We are all unique designs. We have passions and talents and interests and abilities. But we do not possess *all* talents and interests and abilities. You may have many, you do not have all.

You will have to choose. And if I may suggest, it would be best to go with your strengths or as we say at a restaurant, don't order against the house.

At Outback Steakhouse you do not order fish. It's a steakhouse, order the steak. At a seafood restaurant it is best to go with seafood, that's the specialty. At a burger joint, get the burger.

As you cross this threshold, I encourage you to find out what your design is. What are your strengths, your talents, your abilities, your passions? Pursue those.

Do I mean you must be accomplished or skilled already? No! But you have been designed with a purpose, find out what it is. Pursue your possibilities.

The best and most direct place to go to find your unique design is to the designer himself.

Yes, God is real. And he made you. And you have talents and gifts and abilities.

Do those things.

You can't be EVERYTHING. And you really can't be ANYTHING. But you can be THE thing you were designed to be. And when you pursue your designer and his design you will know joy and energy and it will be good.

It will still be hard, and it will still be work, but it will be work that rejuvenates you, not drains you, work that brings fulfillment, not emptiness.

So class of 2010, seek your designer and be what he designed you to be.

Did He Ever Return?

The Kingston Trio, a musical group popular in the 50s and 60s sang a song called M.T.A. (Boston Song). It tells the story of a man who boarded the Boston subway only to discover that the fare had been raised and he was a nickel short and could not get off the train. The song was a protest over increased fares or something, but it was the chorus that echoed in my brain:

> *Did he ever return? No, he never returned,*
> *and his fate is still unlearned.*
> *He may ride forever 'neath the streets of Boston,*
> *he's the man who never returned*[28]

You see, I received a phone call on a Saturday night in August. It was my son. He and two friends were enjoying a long weekend at our cottage in Canada, only now it looked like it might be a longer trip than was first anticipated.

My son had lost his wallet. A tragedy at any time, what with cash, driver's license, and debit card inside. But this was more than a tragedy, this was an international crisis, because along with the aforementioned items, my son lost his passport card.

He was now a Man Without a Country. No ID. No way back into the United States.

What to do? He and his friends spent an entire day searching for the wallet. He even wisely enlisted his Aunt Laurie's help, knowing she possessed the searching skills of a mother. But alas, no wallet.

One of his options was to travel, ever so carefully, to the

capital of Canada and seek help from the American embassy, but instead, he did what every child does when they are lost and in trouble.

He called his parents.

Fortunately for my son, in addition to the lost passport card, he also owned a passport book. It was this book he asked us to deliver to him in Canada.

To travel from Detroit, Michigan to Windsor, Ontario, the Detroit River must be crossed via the Ambassador Bridge. Arrangements were made to meet our Lost Boy in the McDonald's located at the exit of bridge traffic in Windsor.

Larry and I made the trip together, and when asked, as we always are, by the Canadian Border Guard where we were going in Canada, Larry pointed, "To that McDonald's."

The guard raised his eyebrows, McDonalds? There is nothing special about McDonald's in Canada, the exchange rate is not so good that it makes the bridge tolls and sales taxes worth the trip.

So further explanation must be given. We had to explain our dubious errand of delivering a passport to our son.

Perhaps the guard had children of his own, perhaps our faces showed the authentic endurance required on such an errand, whatever the case we were permitted to enter Canada without a full body search.

Larry and I sat down and enjoyed Canadian McDonald sundaes and waited for the arrival of the Man Without a Country. The boys arrived, the exchange was made and all that remained was the return to the U.S. and the necessary explanation of why we had been in Canada for only an hour, and to deliver government documents at that!

Unlike the man beneath the streets of Boston, happily, our son returned.

Was it on the List?

We had made lists. All kinds of lists. And we packed, and packed and loaded the van and off we drove, eight hours to Marquette, Michigan, to deliver our youngest to Northern Michigan University.

We arrived a day early and so were able to relax in our hotel room before calling it a night. It was when we went to turn in that our daughter discovered her retainer case was empty.

And then she remembered. A friend had driven up from Ohio the day before we left to say goodbye. He caught her by surprise, and she was still wearing her retainer. He asked what was on her teeth. Embarrassed, she removed the retainer and folded it into a napkin and set it on the kitchen table.

But where was it now? Was it still there? Was it in the trash? We would have to wait until Larry and I returned home to search.

Upon our return, I had the pleasure of going through the trash in search of the missing oral device.

I wore gloves. This was going to be like a scene out of some investigative TV show like *Bones* or *CSI*.

I searched with great hope the trash still in the house, found plenty of napkins, none holding a retainer. So to the outside trash cans I went.

There were a lot of feral cats in our neighborhood that summer and one of them had caught a bird. I can only surmise the fight that took place over the bird, because the aftermath was bird parts strewn all about my side yard.

I don't do dead. It was up to Larry to seek and find all scattered body parts and deposit them in the trash cans.

I knew those bird parts were still there, so I asked Larry to remove the bags of trash for me. There were only two. This wouldn't be so bad.

It was sunny and bright, if I were actually on the TV show *Bones* it would have been night and I would have been in an alley. But a TV show has no odor and no flies, and I had both, lucky, lucky me.

The first bag did not yield the object of my quest. The second bag was older, and therefore much more disgusting. The further I got into that bag the less I wanted to find the retainer. There was moldy food, soggy napkins, and flies buzzing inside of everything, how *did* they get inside the old food containers?

And then I found it.

Not the retainer. No, this was something I had never seen in person and never need to see again. Maggots. Living maggots. Just like on TV, only right in my face. They are not any better in person.

The quest was over. The retainer would be discovered among her packed belongings or not at all. No way was anyone putting anything from this trash bag in their mouth!

Valentine's Day

Ah Valentine's Day, a day to celebrate love. A day when young people (ok girls) dream that red hearts and chocolate will lead to a white dress and cake.

When a couple becomes engaged the focus shifts, rather radically, from the couple themselves to a day. A single day in the future that begins to take over. A date is chosen, church and hall must be reserved. Invitations selected, colors, themes, music. The DRESS. Entrees, cake, tuxedos, photographer, flowers.

The focus becomes The Wedding. But the wedding lasts only a few hours. It's what is left after the wedding that really requires our focus. The food will be eaten, the music will stop, the flowers will die, the tuxes must be returned, the guests go home, and the dress, the all-important dress will end up in a box somewhere.

What remains after The Wedding? Perhaps the top layer of a cake that will *not* taste good one year later, photos, memories, and...

When my beloved and I were engaged, we went through premarital counseling with our minister. We talked about many things that meant absolutely nothing to us like:

- Finances. What finances? We were broke.

- Communication. I love him, he loves me, what more do we need to talk about?

- Children. Sorry guys but you weren't even a twinkle in Daddy's eye yet.

When we finished talking about marriage, we focused on the truly important thing: The Wedding. We selected music and made some other decisions regarding readings and such. Then we were given a choice regarding our vows.

Vows. Of all the decisions that must be made regarding The Wedding, this should be of greatest importance. What remains after The Wedding?

Promises.

But of course, I am speaking in hindsight.

Writing our own vows was never considered, so we were given a choice between three sets of vows.

One of the promises jumped out at me: I will forgive you as we have been forgiven. I liked that. That brought Jesus right into our Big Day. The deal was done, these would be our vows:

> These things I promise you: I will be faithful to you and honest with you; I will respect, trust, help, and care for you; I will share my life with you; I will forgive you as we have been forgiven; and I will try with you to better understand ourselves, the world, and God; through the best and the worst of what is to come as long as we live.

This we promised each other before our selected witnesses on a beautiful day in October. But what did I know then? At 19 what did I really think "through the best and the worst of what is to come" meant?

A friend lent me Sara Groves' CD *Fireflies and Songs*. On it there is a song about marriage, about two people "loving each other, sharing our secrets, baring our souls, helping each other come clean."[29] But the best line of the whole song is this:

"Better than our promises, is the day we got to keep them."[30]

On my wedding day I did not look ahead and imagine the day I would get to keep my promises.

I could not foresee the best...three beautiful children, good friends, churches, moves, travel.

Nor could I imagine the worst...a miscarried pregnancy, depression, financial stress, job changes, death of a parent, pain that only someone allowed so close can inflict.

I could not foresee the days I would choose to respect my beloved, the days I would trust him, the days I would help him, care for him. I didn't foresee the best or the worst, and I really didn't anticipate having to forgive him as we have been forgiven.

But after The Wedding that is what remains: a man, and a woman, and some promises.

cha·grin (shə-grĭn′)n. A keen feeling of mental unease, as of annoyance or embarrassment, caused by failure, disappointment, or a disconcerting event[31]

Chagrined

I experienced a keen feeling of mental unease as of embarrassment this past weekend.

It was a busy weekend. It was a wedding weekend. My eldest was in town to nail down some of her wedding details. And we would be attending my niece's wedding.

I awoke Sunday, the day of the wedding, to beautiful weather, which is a gift for any bride, but an especially important gift for the bride being married outside.

I was in a good mood and began humming, "*Going to the Chapel...*"[32] I altered the lyrics to say

Going to my niece's cuz she's gonna get married....

Thinking that was rather cheery and clever I decided to post it as my Facebook status.

Once online I visited my niece's wedding website to review some of the unique elements of her wedding ceremony.

This led me to think about what *I* think is the most important part of the ceremony, the vows. A bride and groom are entering a covenant and making promises, and what they promise is important.

That reminded me of the blog I wrote for Valentine's Day 2010. Valentine's Day "when girls dream that red hearts and chocolate will lead to a white dress and cake."

Now I was *very* cheerful, enjoying that turn of phrase and thinking how clever I am. So I added the blog link to my Facebook status about my niece so anyone who hadn't read it would have another chance.

It's a good blog, talking about what remains after the wedding, the promises, and the idea that we really don't go into the wedding day thinking about a future when we will get to *keep* those promises.

Good, thoughtful message.

And I thought to myself, has anyone read this? It's good stuff.

And that's when I felt chagrined. It was the thought that followed that got me. A thought that recognized a parallel possibility. And it was a question as these thoughts often are...

I wonder if God ever feels that way, about his writing - the Bible?

Has anyone read this? It's good stuff.

What is on the To-Do List?

I was focused, very narrowly focused on an event that was nine days away.

It consumed my thoughts, though I greatly desired to give the impression that it did not.

I have always been a list person, because my brain will race faster and faster, in tight circles like NASCARs at Bristol with things I must do, unless I commit them to a list. I have paper and pen ever near me.

Yet even then my brain races. I must review the lists, condense the lists, check off the lists, and when they are messy, I must recopy the lists and then *gasp* throw away the old list. But only after compulsively checking and re-checking that every task made it to the new list.

Why is it that the important things never make it to the list?

You know, the real things. The moments that are real life and not tasks.

My daughter was getting married. In nine days.

Nine. Days.

And my list told me I had...

- Phone calls to make, one to the vet for my dog to get shots (it has to do with the wedding, really)
- People to meet (caterer, baker)
- Information to dispense (187, chicken and sirloin)
- Petals to count (13 orange, 13 ivory)

- A video to create
- Details to organize
- Tasks to delegate
- People to pick up at the airport
- A program to print

Nowhere on my list did I see:

- Laugh with oldest friend and brothers till I pee

Everything was in place. We all had clothing to wear. People would come. Flowers would appear. The photographer would record it. The pastor would officiate the union of my daughter and her beloved. And after that...it's just lunch and icing.

Perhaps it was time for a new list...

- Nap
- Sit still
- Visit with Mom and Dad
- Play fetch with the dog before she goes off to her doggy hotel (hence the shots)
- Reflect on 25 years with my daughter
- Pay Attention
- Move slowly
- Enjoy it all

And most importantly:

- Laugh till I pee
- Repeat

Hello 51

I was driving down Washington Street in Marquette, Michigan, and glanced at the speed limit sign on the right.

Speed limit 50.

I was 50. That was my age then. But in a week I would surrender it. And then the number that represents half a century of life, that freaks out most folks, but that I have embraced – this great number would no longer be mine.

And I would be 51. Nothing very cool about that.

I would be on the Other Side of 50. That's the hill, right? And I'm now over it? On the downward slope?

Fifty years of life, of learning.

I'm still learning. As I move through my life, I frequently discover better ways of doing things. I see places where I thought I was right, but I was wrong. I gain a better understanding of myself, others.

But there is no going back to apply these lessons learned. No do overs. My kids have grown up so the lessons I learned about parenting can only be passed on to those who are parenting growing children now.

In 50 years I made a lot of mistakes. Reflecting on my mistakes regret becomes an unwelcome companion. Like Matthew West sings:

> *Hello my name is Regret.*
> *I'm pretty sure we have met.*

CHOOSING COMEDY

Every day of your life,
I'm the whisper inside
that won't let you forget.[33]

Regret might whisper to Matt West, but it is much bolder with me. It prefers to use memories like postcards and flash the images before my eyes till I cringe, blush from embarrassment or groan with...regret.

Regret over things I have done or said. Mistakes, missteps, miscues. My mistakes devastate me.

A number of years back I attended a leadership conference, and the speaker, Nancy Ortberg, instructed extroverts to write some phrases on a post-it note to keep with them during meetings:

- I was wrong.
- I made a mistake.
- I dropped the ball.
- I'm sorry.
- I don't know, what do you think?

As I listened to this talk for what must be the eighth time, dawning washed over me.

She *assumes* I will be wrong, that I will make a mistake, that I will drop the ball. And yet I will still be there to say I'm sorry.

I will still be there.

She knows I will blow it. She expects I will. And it isn't game ending.

I thought mistakes were game ending! I believed that mistakes were something to be deeply ashamed of, something from which you don't recover.

Yet Nancy was moving on as though mistakes did not bring the world to a screeching halt. As though they were something you point out as you go along. "Yeah, there's a mistake. I'm sorry. And we're walking..."

Is this possible? Can mistakes be, simply, mistakes, and not the crippling events I believed them to be?

Can I ditch regret and its unwelcome version of This is Your Messed-Up Life?

I wonder.

And the Winner Is...

I do a lot of comparison, measuring myself against others. In the game of life how am I doing? Who's winning?

Not me.

I'm not productive enough to be valuable. After all, for most of my adult life I didn't work outside the home. And I could barely manage a house. I'm not a great cook, certainly not a great cleaner. If I could afford household help, I would hire a cook. Someone to plan and prepare meals. I do like eating.

Well eating isn't impressive. Everyone eats.

I look around and see women with cleaner homes, women working. Women doing so much more than I do.

It seems like a matter of capacity, and I don't have much.

Not a lot of capacity.

In the kitchen of life, I am a Dixie cup.

Other people are large mugs, pitchers, coolers. Me? I'm a Dixie cup.

Dixie cups are small, they're not the biggest. They're made of paper, they're not the strongest. But I dream and desire to be the "est."

The prettiest, fastest, smartest, wittiest, kindest, strongest.

I want to be the "est." The best. At *something*. At something I like to do. Something that I admire or enjoy. I want to be the best at something that others will admire.

Because being the best is valued, esteemed, honored. Being the winner is great! First place is the pinnacle, that's the target, the goal. Second place? No one remembers. More painful still, often second place is referred to as first loser.

Ouch.

I want to be a winner.

I think it's pretty universal, this desire to be valued. To be seen. To be appreciated. To be cherished. The desire can be so strong it can be like a hunger. A deep need that drives many of us to chase after worthiness. To compete to be set apart, to be recognized as one who has value.

It is heartbreaking to be eliminated from the running. Early on, the realization came, I am not the prettiest, or the smartest. So, I looked around for something else, another category in which to compete.

I liked to write. With the advent of email, I began to send friends and family funny stories about life with the Schmidts.

We enjoyed some pretty amusing adventures. Well, not all were amusing while they were taking place. Many were amusing only in hindsight, only in the telling. But almost any story can be told with humor after the fact.

So I wrote stories of our life hoping to get a laugh.

My suppressed aspiration? To be a columnist. Erma Bombeck, Anna Quindlen, Leonard Pitts, Mitch Albom, Mike Royko, George Will...these are some of the columnists I have followed over the years. I aspired to join their ranks. But I never finished that degree in journalism. I had three children I wanted to be home with. And I suffered from depression.

My capacity was pretty limited, even if my dreams were not.

I stayed home with my kids. Oh, there were occasional part time jobs mixed in through the years, and a four-year stint on the school board, but for the most part the plan was I stayed home with the kids until they start college, then I would look for work to help pay tuition.

In true sitcom fashion, when the time came to go to work, the job I got was as the finance administrator of my church. Me, with my journalism training, my aspirations to be a columnist, my love of words and analogies...I was hired to crunch numbers.

But it was this ironic twist that gave me my first opportunity to write for an audience larger than my immediate family and a few encouraging friends. I was invited to blog on our church website. A few years later and circumstances prompted me to launch my own personal blog.

Often after I posted a new blog, someone who read it and enjoyed it would say, "You should write."

Um, I just did? And you liked it.

Of course, the encouragement was well intentioned. They wanted me to take it to the next step.

Get in the game.

But by the time I had a blog the game had changed. Newspapers were in decline. Blogs are the new columns and it seems like everyone has one. Anyone can write on the internet. And everyone is. Everyone is writing. And as I read many of these very funny and poignant blogs, I realize, wow, they are really good. Better than me.

I lose.

So many voices. So many bloggers. So much being said. More writers than readers most likely.

What's the point? Why bother? Why add to the pile? Why add another voice? Especially if it can't be the best.

Now what?

Can something have value without being the best?

I am not a gardener, but I like playing in the dirt.

My garden has all kinds of plants. And while my favorite color is yellow, I don't limit my garden to only yellow flowers. I have all manner of plants in my garden, tall white daisies, short yellow primroses, maroon mums that bloom in the fall, purple crocus that are the first to appear in spring, blue forget-me-nots, whose name my mother (a more serious gardener) consistently forgets. I have perennial orange day lilies which bloom for only one day, and annual pink and white impatiens that bloom all summer long. Some flowers with beautiful fragrance, like lilacs, some without, like marigold.

So many colors, so many varieties. They're all so different, and each so beautiful.

I can't name the "best" flower. I like them all.

Likewise, my iPod has a variety of music. Many musicians, many genres.

I don't really know which of the groups have won awards or have been declared the best. I like them for other reasons: the tune, the words. A lot depends on my mood. Do I need some upbeat music to get energized? Or do I need a nice instrumental for contemplating?

What if my iPod was limited to only the *best* singer?

That's it. Only one. But it was the *best* one.

I would be sad if I had to pick only one. Only one singer, or one song.

If flowers and music can have value without being the "best" is it possible that I can too?

Could life be more like my garden or iPod and less of a contest?

The Weekend

CHOOSING COMEDY

Hosanna! Save Us Son of David!

While Jesus was teaching, he would ask the people who came to him, What do you want?

And they would answer...

> ... to see
> ...we brought you our friend so that he might walk
> ...I've bled for 12 years
> ...my child is sick
> ...my brother is dead
> ...we are oppressed by the heathen Romans!

But Jesus responded, Your sins are forgiven.

Our sins?

No, Hosanna! Save us from our pain! Save us from our illness! Deliver us from our circumstances!

Often, we think we know what's happening.
We lean on our own understanding,
rely on our own perspective, only to find out...

We Had No Idea

We knew what every good Hebrew boy knew...we knew God's law; we knew the questions to ask on the night of Passover...we knew Messiah would come and establish David's throne forever.

And like every Hebrew had been asking for hundreds of years we wondered...When would Messiah come?

We had no idea.

When the baptizer was in full swing preaching repentance, turn to God, get ready for the kingdom of God, Andrew was among those following him. But one day John, the baptizer, who seemed like a prophet (and we hadn't seen one of those for a long time) John pointed out another man and said, "He is the one! The one I said was greater than me because he was before me!"

So Andrew followed this new teacher/rabbi, wondering, Who is this man who John says was here before him? We had never heard of him. Who was he?

We had no idea.

When this new rabbi told Peter to go fishing in the morning, the morning! Peter got a little sarcastic and was like, "Ok, Teacher, whatever you say." And then the nets pulled in so many fish it almost sank the boat! It might have if James and

John hadn't pulled alongside. Peter freaked out and fell before Jesus the teacher and said, "Get away from me, I am a sinful man."

Well, sure Peter, you and everyone else, but why did you say that to the teacher? And how did you get so many fish *in the morning?*

We had no idea.

When we were out on the lake and that crazy storm hit, we were sure it was over for us. Yet the rabbi was asleep, in all that weather! Can you imagine? Someone woke him up and he spoke to the storm, the water and the waves, and they calmed. The storm stopped.

Who *does* that? Could this be Messiah?

We had no idea.

James and John thought he was Messiah, in fact, they were so convinced they wanted to secure their place in his new kingdom. So, their mom asked Jesus to put her sons on his right and his left to rule with him.

Nice move dudes. Jesus said those weren't his places to give, but could they drink the cup of suffering?

Suffering? Sure, let me suffer on the right or left hand of the king!

What suffering would Messiah experience?

We had no idea.

When Jesus started talking about all the suffering he would have to endure, Peter tried to set him straight. Messiah suffer? May it never be!

But he was harshly answered, rebuked as a stumbling block to God's ways.

Poor Peter. He put his foot in it that time. So maybe Jesus would suffer, but then, maybe he wasn't the Messiah?

We had no idea.

And then Passover came, and we headed to Jerusalem. To observe the festival and remember when God set his people free from slavery. Wouldn't now be a good time for Messiah to set us free? But when would he come?

We had no idea.

And then Jesus, he does this crazy thing. He rides into Jerusalem on a donkey! Like a king. People lining the street yelling, "Hosanna, Save us!" And he didn't just *agree* to ride into the city on the back of a donkey, he arranged it! He sent a couple of guys to go get the donkey!

What?! Is this it? Is David's throne to be established now once and for all? Freedom from our oppressors! Is Jesus the Messiah? Could it be?

We had no idea.

Then the Passover meal itself. It got a little weird at the end. Jesus was talking about his body and blood. And he offered us a cup, like a man offers a cup to the woman he wants to marry. What did he mean?

We had no idea.

Then it got even weirder. He said someone was going to betray him. What?! *Who?*

We had no idea.

So, there we were, with our teacher, who just rode into Jerusalem like a king, on Passover no less, the perfect time to free God's people. We were on pins and needles, also exhausted. Was this God's time? Was freedom near?

We had no idea.

Then Judas shows up with Roman soldiers and high priests and it looks like a battle is about to erupt. And Peter, ever the first to react, draws his sword and cuts off a kid's ear. But Jesus tells him to put his sword away and *heals* the ear.

And then Jesus goes with the soldiers. He just goes. No fight. No battle. No freedom from slavery on Passover. He just goes with them.

What...?

What happens now?

We had no idea.

The Now and the Not Yet

Friday. Good Friday. It's always seemed odd to call it "good." I look back in history and what I see is that Friday is the day when it all came unraveled.

Twelve young men, some just boys, had spent three years with the Rabbi Jesus. They followed him, learned from him, lived with him, traveled the country with him. They saw him do the miraculous.

He healed people, made eyes see, limbs work, freed people from the bondage of illness, demons. He fed thousands with nothing. He taught them in ways that were confusing. He explained the scripture, the Torah, the prophets in ways that blew their minds.

He commanded the wind to stop. He walked on water. He even raised a man to life who had been dead for three or more days.

Who is this? Who is this rabbi they followed? Is he...? Could he be... the Messiah? The one they have been waiting for?

Imagine living with this man for three years. This *man* who seemed more like God.

Miracles. Healing. Teaching.

What comes next?

Will he overthrow the Romans? Will he restore Israel to a sovereign nation? Will he be king?

And then comes Friday. And he is killed.

Killed. Dead.

Now what?

Life sometimes feels like a season of Good Fridays, one after the other. Anticipation, expectation, hopes, dreams and then hopes and dreams are dashed. Destroyed.

Now what?

I have experienced seasons that seem like on-going Good Fridays. Everything is unraveled.

But.

My seasons of Good Friday all come after.

After what?

Silent Saturday

What happened on Saturday? The day after Jesus was killed on an execution stake? There are several days of events that lead up to the resurrection of Jesus. They have names: Palm Sunday, Maundy Thursday, Good Friday, Easter Sunday.

What happened Saturday?

Nothing.

We are not told anything about Saturday. That long day between Jesus' death and resurrection.

I imagine we are not told anything because those who followed Jesus could not *do* anything.

The women who had come with Jesus from the Galil followed Joseph and saw the tomb and how his body was placed in it.[34] But the Sabbath was about to begin. They went back home to prepare spices and ointments. On the Sabbath the women rested, in obedience to the commandment.

The women who followed Jesus, who loved Jesus, had to wait. They had to rest. They could not attend to Jesus' body and prepare it properly for entombment. They could not work on the Sabbath. So they waited.

They could not stay busy to distract themselves from their grief. They had to be still and wait in their pain.

When tragedy strikes, I am stunned. I am left with questions like: What do I do now?

What do I *DO* now?

114

When I am in pain and grieving, I often begin to move fast, to occupy myself with something.

The followers of Jesus couldn't do that.

It was the Sabbath. The day of rest.

There were very clear restrictions on what activity was permitted before it began to be "work." Work was not permitted.

The day after Jesus was killed, his followers could not do anything. They made sure his body was in a grave before the sun set Friday night. And then they couldn't do anything.

They couldn't properly prepare his body.

They couldn't run.

They couldn't lose themselves in work.

They had to be still. Be still. Rest. Wait.

They didn't know what was coming next.

I sense this was very carefully orchestrated by God. Jesus' friends experienced the worst tragedy. They suffered the death of the one they loved, the one they followed, the one they had put their hope in. The one they may have dared to believe was more than just a man like them.

He is dead.

Now what?

Now nothing. It is the Sabbath. Rest. Be still.

Silent Saturday.

It is something to think about the next time the worst possible thing happens. When tragedy strikes and the question is: What do I do now? Maybe the initial answer should be...nothing.

I imagine that is what Jesus' friends did Saturday.

Nothing. Just stayed together, quietly, being scared, sad.

Remember, they had no idea what Sunday was bringing.

Sunday

The men and women who followed Jesus had to live through Good Friday and Silent Saturday without knowing. They didn't know.

They didn't know about Sunday.

Sunday when the tomb is found to be empty.[35]

Sunday when Jesus is seen, *alive*.

Sunday when joy and hope and understanding explode and blow away all sorrow and confusion and grief.

Sunday when the pieces begin to fall into place.

They didn't know what happened. But I do. And it changed everything. Backwards and forwards. Sunday changed everything.

Everything.

And I live after. All my seasons of difficulty, of devastation, come after the resurrection. I know.

I know the victory is won. I know there is forgiveness. I know there is freedom. I know this Rabbi Jesus is a man *and* God.

But there's more.

I live after Sunday, but there's more to come. The hope of living in his presence without any trace of sin, death, pain. I live after Sunday- the Now. But I look forward to the rest- the Not Yet.

CHOOSING COMEDY

Tell Me What It Looks Like

CHOOSING COMEDY

Kintsugi

Pottery is an art that gives us objects both beautiful and useful.

These objects are also fragile. When they break, they are no longer useful. And in so many pieces they are not terribly beautiful either.

That is where I often live. In brokenness, unable to see any beauty. And in today's culture broken things are disposed of, thrown out. Broken things are garbage.

In ancient Japan, however, a choice was made to repair broken pottery, and the resulting art form is called Kintsugi which means "golden joinery."[36] The pottery was mended by mixing lacquer with powdered precious metals, like gold. The pieces are placed back together and repaired with seams of gold.

The result is a vessel that is restored to its original form. But its brokenness shows. Every crack and seam stand out in shiny precious metal.

The brokenness, the places where it was shattered still show. And it's beautiful. Beautiful and more valuable than it was before.

It's beautiful?

About a week after Jesus' resurrection, the disciples were gathered together. Many of them had seen Jesus alive. Thomas had not.

Thomas was not convinced Jesus was alive again. He told his

friends, "Unless I see the nail marks in his hands, put my finger into the place where the nails were and put my hand into his side, I refuse to believe it."[37]

Thomas had been with Jesus almost three years. He knew him very well. And he knew that Jesus died.

Thomas knew that his teacher, his rabbi Jesus was broken, broken and killed. And unless he saw the brokenness, he would not believe it was Jesus, would not believe he was alive.

Although the doors were locked, Jesus came, stood among them and said, "Peace to you all!"

Then he said to Thomas, "Put your finger here, look at my hands, take your hand and put it into my side."[38]

There was Jesus, alive, with his scars.

Jesus was risen from the dead, but his scars remained on his body. In the book of Revelation John relates seeing a vision of Jesus in heaven and Jesus looks like a lamb that was slain.

Jesus will have these scars forever.

Thomas answered, "My Lord and my God!"

Jesus said to him "Have you trusted because you have seen me? How blessed are those who do not see, but trust anyway!"[39]

I Can't See

Flying back from Florida my plane was preparing to land in some very thick fog.

When flying I am a wee bit tense on take-off, and a wee bit tense on landing, and definitely tense if there is a lot of turbulence. But this particular landing really caught my attention because I couldn't see anything.

Looking out the window I saw a wall of cloud. There was no visibility. I wondered, are we flying at the right altitude? At the right speed?

I was disoriented so I worried the pilot would be too. I couldn't affirm that the pilot was doing well because I couldn't see.

The thing is, I don't actually know what the pilot should be doing. I don't know what the approach speed of an airplane is supposed to be. I don't know what the altitude should be.

My seeing or not seeing made no difference. Because I don't actually know how to fly a plane.

Recently a group of friends were talking together about life and the issue of people wanting to fix things, wanting to fix other people's lives.

One friend observed, "I can't fix it. I can't put it back together, because I don't know what it's supposed to look like in the first place."

He's right. I don't know what it's supposed to look like either. I arrived on the scene after everything was broken. I can only imagine what the pre-broken world was like. And even then, my imagination fails me.

Trying to put the pieces back together I have no idea where they go, and there is no puzzle box top for reference.

In fact, my instinct is to hide brokenness. I work hard to appear unbroken, to try and keep it all together by myself.

But all the king's horses and men and I, we can't put it back together again,

Only the king, the potter, the one who designed it all in the first place, only he knows what it's supposed to look like. Only he can make the golden repairs and restore the vessels to beauty and purpose.

It's Worth *What?*

My husband and I visited Domino's Farms in Ann Arbor, Michigan, back when it was still owned by Tom Monaghan. Monaghan kept some of his classic car collection there.

There was one car we saw, and Larry, a car guy through and through, asked me, "How much do you think that car is worth?" I didn't know. Larry said, "$1,000,000."

Really?

I saw a car. Simply a car. Made up of different parts, the sum of which – not being made of gold or platinum – would not add up to $1,000,000. A *million dollars.*

How was that value determined?

And it hit me.

The car was worth a million dollars, because that is the price Tom Monaghan was willing to pay for it. He wanted the car. He wanted the car and so he was willing to pay $1,000,000 for it.

Value is determined by what someone is willing to pay.

God wanted me.

Me, with my limited capacity, without a college degree, without a lifelong career, without having been declared the "best" in any category. How can something have value without being the best?

God wanted me, broken though I am.

The one who created me, is also the one who, after I was lost to him, paid a high price to get me back. A very high price.

God loved me so much he gave his only son for me. Jesus gave his life to get me back.

Jesus laid down his life for me.

That is how my value is determined.

And yours.

What Good is a Dixie Cup?

My dear friend, the Horse Whisperer, also teaches. I was in one of her classes and we were considering how we view things and the old question was posed...

Is the glass half empty or half full?

I said that I never really thought about it in those terms, I saw the cup and my thought was: It can hold more.

There is the potential for the cup to hold more.

That cup is not living up to its potential. It should hold more. Kind of like I saw myself. I should do more. I'm not living up to my potential.

But my friend *really* thought outside the box.

She considered the cup and said, "I would ask a question, 'What is it for?' If it is here to quench my thirst as I'm talking, we're good. But if it's here to put out a fire, we don't have nearly enough."

What's it for?

What am I for?

If I'm a Dixie cup...what am I for? I'm really asking, what am I good for? What good is a cup this small, this limited?

Well, a Dixie cup can refresh one person at a time.

But if I try to water the lawn with a Dixie cup, I'm going to get tired.

Really tired. I know. I've tried.

To water the lawn, a garden hose is needed.

Yet if I try to get a drink from a garden hose, well, I can, but it's not very efficient.

So, a Dixie cup. It has a purpose. It has a place.

A Dixie cup has value.

Tattoos

When my three children were born, they were each beautiful and tiny and, I thought, perfect.

I saw them as spotless sheets of paper, without fold, crinkle, blemish.

And I quaked, fearful I was going to really mess them up.

And in many ways, I did, sometimes without realizing, and sometimes because I am the monster at the end of the book.

But I learned that they didn't really arrive as spotless sheets of paper. They came pre-messed up because they came broken.

The fall impacted all of us.

Still, when my youngest informed us that she wanted to get a tattoo, I immediately reverted to the clean sheet of paper vision and balked.

"Mark up this precious body? With permanent ink? Never!"

Or at least, not until you are an adult and I have no say.

When she became an adult her desire for a tattoo had not abated. So I did what any reasonable mom would do, I helped her design it.

If my baby, my child with beautiful, young skin is going to mark it up, well then let's be sure it's a good design, and placed well, and as small as I can influence her to make it.

Turns out not that small.

129

Her father and I went with her for her first tattoo (yes more followed). It was a good experience.

Tattoos are so very common now. I suppose I'm the last generation that viewed them as questionable, only for "ne'er do wells."

My youngest challenged us, what would your tattoo be if you were going to get one?

Huh

I was stumped. What would I want to have on my body forever? This is more permanent than a bumper sticker. I don't even have those. It would have to be something pretty significant.

I couldn't come up with anything.

My husband did.

His tattoo, if he ever got one, would say: Relentlessly Pursued.

That is what we all are, pursued by a loving God who is relentless. Pursued by God who stopped at nothing to reach us and reconcile us to himself.

God who loved us enough to deign to live as one of us. To live here in the brokenness, to make a way out of the brokenness for us all.

We are relentlessly pursued.

And I have been caught.

I'm Never Gonna Get this Right

I'm not going to get anything right. Not really. And that is a very difficult tension to exist in.

Right is what I want to be. I want to get it right.

I get frustrated with myself for missing it. For blundering, screwing up, choosing wrongly.

In Kentucky one summer I walked some kids through an activity that I hoped would help them understand more about God.

I don't know what it did for them, but for myself, I keep learning from this crazy exercise.

We painted a maze on the grass. The kids were paired up. One was blindfolded. The other "talked" them through the maze to a basket of candy. The blindfolded child picked up two candy bars and was guided back out by the directions of their partner.

There were several sets of partners, and they all began at a different place on the maze and all went through it at the same time.

There were so many things I wanted them to experience.

I wanted them to be aware of the need to discern between all the voices calling out. All the noise. Which voice is guiding you? Which voice are you listening to?

I wanted them to trust the voice guiding them. To understand that trusting involves more than an intellectual assent, "Yes, I

hear you. I am sure you are telling me the right thing to do."
Trusting means I have to do it.

I didn't expect the complete and utter trust they put in their
partner - to the extent of crashing into one another at their
partners' directions, not on purpose mind you. But even after
impact they still trusted and followed their partner's voice.

I also didn't expect what happened with the youngest group.
These kids didn't know their left from their right. So how
would they give directions to their partner about where to go?

You go before them. This little girl was five? Six? On her own
she stood a couple steps in front of her even younger partner
and said, "Come to my voice." As her blindfolded partner
stepped toward her, she moved further and repeated, "Come
to my voice."

Wow.

I can picture the kids, calling out directions, "Turn right,"
"Take two steps," "Turn left," "Take five steps."   Many times
the guiding partner said it wrong or the blindfolded partner
did it wrong. But none of them ever stopped. They didn't
agonize over their errors. When a mistake was identified it
was simply corrected, "Oh no, go back three steps." "I meant
left, no your other left..."

No matter what mistakes they made, they kept on, kept
striving, kept moving toward candy bars melting in the
Kentucky heat.

I am pressing on to such a better goal than melted chocolate.

Yet, I become paralyzed. Is it right or left? What should I do?

What if I'm wrong?! Oh no!

I've made a mistake, I've blown it, arghhhh my life is ruined.

But maybe it's just, No, your other left.

Just Walk

There was a man named Peter. He had a wife and a mother-in-law. He made his living fishing with his brother.

One day God came into his life and said, Follow Me. And Peter did.

He followed Jesus.

They walked all over Israel. And some scenes from their journey have been written down.

Peter was a man of enthusiasm, impulse, passion and ideas. But a lot of his ideas were way off track. Peter didn't realize that. He thought they were great ideas.

Peter was the kind of guy who jumped in (or out as the case may be) without thinking a lot first.

So as he walked with Jesus he had some good days and some bad days.

I read about Peter's life and I see a transformation. Peter grew in his understanding of God and he became more and more faithful to serving God.

Like Peter, God has invited me to follow him.

But here's the thing. I thought when I followed Jesus that I would pick up where Peter left off. As though knowing Peter's story somehow imbued me with wisdom from all the mistakes he made and the lessons he learned.

I thought that was why those stories were recorded. Peter

once got out of a boat and walked on water, for a short distance. When he took his eyes off Jesus he sank. Jesus picked him up and asked why Peter didn't trust him.[40]

I always thought I was supposed to read that and when my turn came, I would get out of a boat and dance along, knowing I could trust Jesus.

It hasn't worked out that way.

Apparently, I have to undergo my own transformation.

Instead of picking up where Peter left off, I am living my own life, making my own blunders, sinking in my own lack of trust.

I am sometimes impulsive, ready to run on ahead, prepared to tell Jesus how it's gonna go, and usually I fail miserably along the way.

But this is what I see.

I see Jesus loving Peter. No matter what.

No matter that he couldn't trust Jesus enough to have fun on the water.

No matter that he said some stupid things on a mountain about building tents, like he knew what was needed.

No matter that he told Jesus his plan was bad, and Peter wasn't gonna let it happen.

No matter that he denied knowing Jesus.

All of that, and Jesus still loved him. And Peter walked alongside him.

So this is what I take away from Peter's life. He and I are a lot alike - in the worst of ways. Knowing about Peter's walk doesn't mean I get to skip all my own embarrassing blunders. It doesn't mean I won't make similar mistakes during my own painful transformation.

But Jesus is going to love me through it all.

So, I'll walk, just walk.

Butterflies

I have been thinking a lot about change. But not just change like changing your clothes or your hair color. I have been thinking about transformation. A change so significant that what once was is no more. Being changed from the very depth of my being.

Like a caterpillar becoming a butterfly. How different they are! They look different, they function differently. One day a round, wingless, multi-legged, crawling, worm-like creature. And then the transformation into a sleeker, winged, delicate, colorful, flying, flower-like creature.

As I understand it, I am undergoing a transformation. I will change from a person who puts self first, who thinks she knows more than anyone else, who hurts others, into a person who puts others first, who is humble, who brings healing. A person who resembles God.

Sometimes it seems impossible. How can I be transformed into a person like Jesus?

But there it is. We know caterpillars do transform into butterflies. They go into their cocoons and undergo the most amazing transformation imaginable.

That is some significant body changing going on. That's not a makeover, that is total body reconstruction. Like dying and being reborn as something totally different.

I wonder, does it hurt?

When Jesus invites me to follow him, he says I am to deny myself, pick up my cross and follow him.[41] It's an invitation to a transformation that involves death and rebirth.

I personally find the transformation process to be a painful experience. The process of self, the flesh, the old nature dying and me being reborn as someone entirely different, someone like Jesus.

Self dies hard. In my mind self dying looks like that scene at the end of the movie *Terminator 2*,[42] in which the second terminator is in the molten steel, and he thrashes around fighting it to the last.

I thrash around too.

So I look at the butterfly and wonder, does it hurt?

I think it must.

But, wow, was it worth it.

What Am I Holding?

I am home sick. I've been in bed a few days now. And I have a lot of time to think. To think and to observe. And there is a lot of loss going on around me.

So many good-byes. So many changes. So many things I must let go of.

I want to hold on. Cling tight. I am afraid of losing hold, losing touch, losing all I know, knew, love, loved, all my past.

I hold things close. I value them. Sometimes I don't know how much I value them until I lose them.

I take things for granted. Then I re-evaluate, and try to be present, intentional, in the moment, see everything. Not take today, this moment, this present for granted. For it too will pass on. Change will come.

Did I appreciate it? Value it? Recognize it?

Will I survive the loss?

Often, I am afraid I will not survive the loss. I hold things tighter.

What am I holding onto? What is in my hand? What am I clutching?

Why?

Why am I holding it? Cherishing it? Clinging to it?

Does it warrant being valued above all else?

I am offered the greatest gift ever.

I am offered reconciliation with the God of the universe, the God who is the intelligent designer, the power behind the cosmos.

I am offered forgiveness. And freedom.

And I need both. Forgiveness. And freedom.

I have felt the need for forgiveness, the sense that I have blown it. Completely. How do I recover? How do I get through this mess, guilt, disaster? How do I rise again from these ashes? How do I escape this prison?

By accepting the gift. The gift of forgiveness and reconciliation.

I will need both hands to receive the gift.

Both hands to take hold of it.

Which means I must let go of everything I am holding.

Everything.

I want to bring the gift into my life. Add it to the pile of things I am currently holding.

C.S. Lewis wrote an incredible book – The Great Divorce,[43] telling the story of a bus ride from hell to heaven. Everyone is welcome to stay. But in order to stay they must lay down whatever it is they are holding.

Remarkably, they cannot. They cannot release those things

which keep them chained to hell.

Hell!

They trade away the opportunity of life, light, forgiveness, reconciliation, God. They trade God for whatever it is they are holding.

So easy to see in someone else's life.

So hard to see in my own.

What am I holding that I value more than God?

My stuff? My identity? My sense of self? My pride? My sense of independence? My lifestyle? My family? My loves? My passion?

I am offered the greatest gift. Forgiveness, reconciliation, new life.

It is not a gift that goes on top of the pile of gifts.

It is a gift to be received with both hands.

After I put everything else down.

Where the Rubber Meets the Road

I have learned a lot about God over the years. And I trust what I have learned. I trust that God is good. I trust that he loves me. I trust that he is wise. These are things I know about God and his character. I share these truths with people when they are hurting, or confused, or questioning. A lot of people I love are hurting right now.

So I share what I know. But knowing shouldn't be confused with living.

It is important to know what you believe. That is why we study, talk about, listen to, and chew over God's word. We grow as we learn more and more about God's character and our relationship to him. And that's good. But that's not where it ends.

Eventually we all have to live what we have learned. Walk through what we understand. Can we live with what we know and understand?

Or more importantly, can we live with what we don't know and don't understand?

I've learned that there is a **big** difference between knowing, seeing, and living.

I *know* about tornadoes. I understand what they are, and what they do. I have heard stories of the destruction, the loss, sometimes the death. I have seen photos. I know and I could tell you about tornadoes.

But there is a difference...

A difference between knowing what a tornado is capable of and *seeing* a place that has been struck by a tornado.

To see the destruction firsthand. To walk through a yard where a house once stood. To look up at sharp sticks that were once trees but are now stripped of leaves and branches. Turning in circles seeing the intimate pieces of lives strewn about in the open. This is different than knowing about tornadoes through stories or photos.

And still there is a difference...

There is a difference between *seeing* tornado damage in person and *living* through one. Watching the clouds form. Tracking the radar. Responding to the sirens. Huddling together while the wind creates a noise and force beyond imagination. Hearing windows smash. Feeling the house tremble, shake, give way.

There is a difference between *knowing, seeing* and *living*.

I find it easy to trust what I know about God in the abstract.

It can be more difficult to trust God when I see hardship firsthand.

But can I trust God while I *live* difficulty, pain, hurt?

That is where the rubber meets the road.

Rough Roads Ahead

God rarely reveals the road ahead. We walk without seeing, like the kids blindfolded in the maze. The only way to do that is to stick close to him, listening carefully for God's voice.

I can't see where I'm going, but I walk with God.

I often ask: What is ahead? Where does this lead? How is it all going to work out? But the answer is usually, keep your eyes on me.

This idea of keeping my eyes on Jesus. This is key. This is how I keep going where I should be going. How do I know this? Driving.

How I drive impacts others. Sometimes it literally impacts others. I have worked hard this week to not be impacted by other drivers. Perhaps they weren't paying attention or made a bad judgment call, and I had to do some quick maneuvering to avoid contact.

My driver's education teacher was a man called Mr. Martin. He was a nervous man who had a brake on the passenger side of the car. And he wasn't afraid to use it. I told him he was paranoid once and he vehemently denied it.

Then he asked what paranoid meant.

I called him paranoid decades before I ever attempted to teach my own kids to drive.

Well Mr. Martin if you were afraid, it probably wasn't paranoia, it was probably valid fear! Teaching teens to drive is no task for the faint of heart.

So, thanks. Your driving lessons have come in very handy, on the road and off.

In drivers' education, when I was learning how to handle a monster of a machine, Mr. Martin taught me to look ahead in a curve or turn, because my hands would steer where my eyes were looking.

I tried it and it was like magic! I didn't have to guess how much to turn the steering wheel at every point in the turn, if I kept my eyes on the road ahead, my hands steered me there almost without thinking!

Of course, the opposite is also true: If I look away from the road, my hands will steer me the direction my eyes are looking. Thank you rumble strips for keeping me in my lane!

Keeping my eyes on Jesus I will walk toward him.

Mapping a Route to Something Precious

I am from the Motor City, and I live with a Car Guy. Cars are a big deal here. Yet it may be one of the most difficult places to learn how to drive. Detroit is a city with lots of freeways, and very large surface roads. So large they are often boulevards, four lanes of traffic going in either direction with some green space in between.

You cannot just turn left at any given intersection. Frequently, if you want to go left, you must first turn right.

That's right. To get to where you want to be you must first turn away from it, completely, go in the exact opposite direction. Then, after a bit, you will be able to turn back to your intended destination.

I have been considering my destination and the path that must be traveled. A path that is often difficult. A rough road.

For instance, in Paul's letter to the believers in Rome, we are given the route to hope.

Here are the directions: Start with suffering, which will lead you to perseverance, which leads to character, which leads to hope.[44]

That's right, the road to hope begins with suffering. Suffering? That's where we start? AAA could never get away with this map. Suffering? Perseverance? Where's the scenic route?

James opens his letter to the 12 tribes scattered among the nations in this way:

146

> *My friends, consider yourselves fortunate when all kinds of*
> *trials come your way, for you know that when your faith*
> *succeeds in facing such trials, the result is the ability to*
> *endure. Make sure that your endurance carries you all the*
> *way without failing, so that you may be perfect and*
> *complete, lacking nothing.*[45]

When my faith succeeds in facing trials? Another way to say
that would be to use the definition of faith[46] found in the
book of Hebrews: When my assurance of things I hope for
and my certainty of things I can't see succeed in facing
difficulties like frustration, pressure, and irritation, the result
will be endurance, perseverance.

In college some Christ followers I knew often talked about
the crowns they would have at the end of life to offer to Jesus.
They encouraged each other that obedience now would
translate into jewels in a crown that they would someday offer
to Jesus as they worshiped him.[47]

As I reflect on that now it is interesting, the process through
which some jewels are made. Like say diamonds or pearls.

God chose to form diamonds with sustained pressure.
Unbelievable pressure over a very long time. That is how
carbon becomes a diamond, a tough and beautiful stone.

And then there are pearls. Pearls are the result of something
foreign entering an oyster. This foreign matter is often a small
piece of sand, but it is very irritating to the oyster. And it
doesn't go away.

The oyster secretes something over a very long period of time
that covers the irritant until the final result is a pearl.
Pressure and irritants?

Time to count the cost. I have to decide if I really want to go with God. Can I trust him to be my guide? Can I trust him when life is filled with suffering? Can I trust him to determine not only the destination, but the route?

It's a serious question. Will I go all in? It means surrendering a lot.

No, actually it means surrendering everything.

I may see some nice spots along the way, but I may not get to visit them.

Can I acknowledge that I am not and will never be in control?

Jesus says he is the way (route), the truth (reality) and the life.[48]

I could try another route, or seek another reality, but to turn away from life leaves only death.

So I will consider it pure joy, when life presses in on me, or irritants plague me, for when my certainty of God's love and my assurance of his sovereignty succeeds in facing the stress and irritants, the result will be diamonds and pearls. But I must make sure that my endurance carries me all the way, I must persevere to the end.

If I spit out that irritating piece of sand, or if I dodge the pressure, the result will be that I remain an empty oyster or a lump of coal.

Pulling a Peter

I've been doing my imitation of the apostle Peter, and not his good side. When Jesus told Peter to come to him on the water, Peter did. But that's not the Peter I've been imitating lately. I'd like to get to the part where I climb out of the boat toward Jesus, he's certainly waiting for my response.

My response to what? To the question. *The* question. The one I keep trying to answer verbally, but it just doesn't work that way.

I've been a bit melancholy lately, and I'm not very comfortable with melancholy.

So I will do just about anything to shake it. I will stand outside in the cold with my face to the sun hoping that the right sunlight waves will kick in my Vitamin D. I will ride my exercise bike for 30 minutes chasing after some exercise endorphins. I am less inclined to try chocolate these days; it seems to hang around longer and longer.

If the melancholy persists, I begin looking around at other people, and here's where my imitation of Peter kicks in: What about him Lord? What about her? Why are they (fill in the blank) and I'm not?

That's what Peter did on the beach after Jesus rose from the dead. Jesus was giving Peter a peek into what his future held—ironic isn't it?

I will clamor for knowledge of my future from God. What's ahead? I demand. Well, Jesus was telling Peter what was ahead, and Peter wasn't all that thrilled, so he looked around, spotted John and asked Jesus, "What about him?"[49]

Not his finest moment. Not mine either.

And that's when the question comes in. God asks us all the question. The question that will not accept a verbal response.

The best picture of this question and the answer is from Disney's *Aladdin*.[50] The young Aladdin asks Princess Jasmine twice, "Do you trust me?" The first time he asks, he is about to jump off a great height. She must make a decision; does she trust him? She takes his hand and jumps with him.

The second time he is standing on a magic carpet and he reaches out to her, "Do you trust me?" And again, she must decide, Do I trust him? Again, she takes his hand.

Simply saying "yes" will not suffice. Giving a verbal answer is no answer at all. If there is trust, then Jasmine follows Aladdin.

If I trust God I must get out of the boat.

If I trust God, I must take his hand and walk with him.

If I trust God, I must do it.

God is holding out his hand, asking, Do you trust me?

> *I will trust God by taking his hand*
> *I won't rely on my own understanding*
> *I will accept the truth of God,*
> *And he will guide me*[51]

How Does It End?

CHOOSING COMEDY

Jesus Wants What?

When I look at Jesus' life, sometimes it feels like I am following a crazy man. I mean the stuff he says...

- If someone takes your shirt give him your coat too.[52]
- If someone imposes on you, go an extra mile.[53]
- Do good to your enemies.[54]

Now, he doesn't really mean those things...there are qualifications, right? Questions that must be asked and answered?

I mean what's going to happen if I start giving stuff to everyone who asks? How are they going to learn to take care of themselves? I might end up with nothing. What will that accomplish?

Who are my enemies? Irritating people or *real* enemies? How am I supposed to do good to my real enemies? I could get hurt. I don't know how someone is going to respond. I will be vulnerable. What will that accomplish?

I just have to look at Jesus' life to see he doesn't want me to be as crazy as some of this stuff sounds, right? I mean, when people hurled accusations at him, when people struck him, when one of his closest friends betrayed him how did he respond?

He was Messiah, the Son of God, if he let his enemies walk all over him how would they know who he was?

If he died, what would that accomplish?

Even Peter knew better.

Jesus told his followers the Son of Man must die. Peter said, No Way!

Jesus answered, Get behind me Satan.[55]

Peter knew who Jesus was, he was the Messiah, the Jews would be saved by Messiah. But if Messiah dies, well, it's game over. Sure, he can heal people and raise other people from the dead. But if he's dead, there's no doing anything. He's dead.

If Messiah dies what does that accomplish?

Everything.

Peter just didn't know. Couldn't grasp the whole concept. Couldn't wrap his mind around how Jesus dying was going to help anything. He truly thought it was game over.

Jesus knew it wasn't.

God the Father sent Jesus. Jesus knew the plan ahead of time. Still when the time came Jesus asked, *Is there another way?*[56]

He wrestled with his father and then moved out in obedience. And he did some pretty crazy stuff.

Jesus did good to his enemies. He did not strike back. He did not go down fighting.

Spit upon. Nothing.

Beaten. Nothing.

Yelled at, mocked. Nothing.

Put on a cross to die, now Jesus finally says something, Father, forgive them they do not know what they are doing.[57]

Jesus died. Peter and the others thought it was game over. Nothing was accomplished. Evil won.

And then came Sunday. Jesus is alive. *Alive?*

Who saw that coming? No one. Certainly not the women who were coming to prepare his dead body for a proper burial. And not the disciples who were in hiding, pretty sure they were next on the enemy's list.

Who saw the resurrection coming? Jesus did. He knew. Peter had no clue.

So now I am faced with my own cross, which I am told to take up and follow Jesus. I am told to love my enemies. Love them. Serve them. Feed and refresh them.

Loving my enemies seems crazy. But I am told to do these things because that's how God wants me to live.

What will that accomplish?

Two things:

First, If I love Jesus I will do what he told me to do.

Doing these stupid things reveals my love for Jesus. This is what I was created for. I will be doing what I was created to do.

Second, well, I have no idea. I don't.

The disciples had no idea what Jesus' death would accomplish. And it accomplished everything. Everything. So what will my obedience to Jesus accomplish? I have no idea.

But if I don't live that way, if I don't follow Jesus in these crazy things...then I don't follow Jesus.

Go, Jesus said. Go into all the world and make disciples baptizing them in my name [58] Go

And be prepared to give up everything. Leave behind everything.

Did I think he was exaggerating? Or that he didn't mean me?

It all started with a Bible study called Men's Fraternity. Larry listened. And he talked to the other guys on Tuesday mornings for three years. And he started thinking about his life. His life divided up in thirds.

The first third, he didn't even know Jesus.

The second third, he poured himself into our family, raising our kids.

And now he was on the threshold of what, God willing, would be one third more of life.

He began to hear the quiet voice of God. And he began to get a picture of what this final third of life could look like. How it could be spent in ways that would yield eternal fruit. And we started talking. And it was exciting. God had plans. But they weren't going to start right away, because our kids were not fully on their own yet. But soon. Very soon.

And our church, where I worked, where we raised our kids, where we worshiped and grew for over 20 years, Grace Chapel, planted Mercy Road in our hometown.

And we were excited! Great! Redford needs this! Yes! We will help as much as we can, but of course we won't leave Grace.

So there was Larry, serving part time at Mercy Road and part time at Grace. And I was serving overtime at Grace.

And Larry wants to worship together again. But he misses Mercy Road when he's not there. So maybe he'll keep his fingers in the Mercy Road pie and Grace too.

But that's not an option. God wants Larry All In. At Mercy Road.

And so Larry comes to me and says, for your sake I would stay at Grace. And we realize he has been Jonah, ignoring God for many months for my sake.

How absolutely ridiculous are we?

That we thought God wanted us at Mercy Road did not come as a big surprise to our kids, "Isn't that what Doug has been preaching for years? Go into your neighborhoods with the gospel?" our son asked.

But it was a surprise to me. The bigger surprise, however, was my emotional reaction. I didn't want to leave Grace Chapel.

I wasn't being asked to go to another country, or serve in a foreign culture, where I didn't know the language.

I was asked to go to my hometown. How selfish am I?

Jesus wanted Larry and I to take the good news of salvation in Jesus to the people in our neighborhood whom we have known for years. Jesus wanted us to work in Redford alongside other believers we have known for years.

I had been writing blogs for Grace Chapel's blog *Graceworks* for several years at this point. I read back over them all.

I know I enjoyed a rather small readership. And from those who read my blogs, I hadn't had much feedback. Sometimes I wondered if anyone was paying attention.

Re-reading the blogs I got the distinct impression that God had been wondering the same thing.

About me.

All these great little bits of truth and pieces of the picture he has given me over the years, and I think he's wondering, Were you paying attention?

Not as much as I thought, I guess.

I'm embarrassed by how I felt. I cried. I grieved. I felt like my whole life was being turned upside down and ripped apart. And I didn't know what would be left.

As it turns out what was left was the truth that apart from Jesus, I am ***not*** a "nice person who occasionally does bad things."

Apart from Jesus I am a selfish person who occasionally does good things and is darn proud of them.

What is left is the gospel. The truth that I am completely corrupt and owe God a debt I cannot pay. Jesus paid it for me. And having received his righteousness, his life, I am being transformed. And while that transformation takes place, I will take the gospel to Redford.

I will do that because Jesus lives in me, not because I am anything at all. I'm not. I proved that pretty well. I hope I will remember, but I will probably forget again.

The truth I share about Jesus is the truth *I* need, every day.

Thank God he is willing to remind me.

Knitting

My grandma taught herself to knit left-handed so she could teach me, because I am left-handed. But I never became proficient.

I know the difference between knit and pearl. And I know what you have to do when you've made a mistake...you unravel all your work back to that mistake and start again.

New yarn off the skein is straight. Yarn that has been knitted and unraveled has a curliness to it.

I feel that I am in a season of unraveling. Taking apart, deconstructing what is, until we can get back to the mistake.

Right now, I am working backwards to a flaw in my expectations and definitions.

I expected my life to go a certain way. To proceed at a certain pace, along a particular path.

When those expectations weren't met there was confusion, disappointment, and a certain amount of self-contempt.

I think I got it wrong.

While raising my kids I read a lot of books. Generally, by people who had raised their own kids. There was a lot of information, but it didn't always co-exist nicely, a lot of times the "experts" were in conflict.

Between the mountain of information from child raising experts and my kids' cries of "it's not fair" I learned something.

There was always a goal. I was always working toward something.

Sometimes my goal was to achieve peace and quiet.

Sometimes it was a very low bar - keep the kids alive.

But at its core my ultimate goal for each of my kids was that they become emotionally healthy adults who follow Jesus.

Moving toward that goal did not look the same for each one.

After all, if one was sick, they didn't all go to the doctor. If one broke a bone, they didn't all get casts.

It wasn't the same and it didn't seem fair. But to the best of our ability we tried to give each child what they needed, to move them toward our ultimate goal.

Books on child raising or discipleship can lean one of two ways, toward method or principle.

Methods are attractive because I tend to prefer lists, clear instructions: Do This. But methods have drawbacks, they are not one size fits all and eventually the method fails me.

Principles can be discouraging because they are more of a compass than a map.

An arrow pointing off into the general direction, leaving a lot of latitude in how to proceed in that general direction.

Too much latitude. I am not always comfortable with too much left to my discretion. I desire clear instruction, detailed to-do lists, something I can check off, measure progress by.

How will I know if I'm getting it right?

The thing is we were created to be in relationship. First in relationship with God, and then in relationship with others.

Relationships are messy. And really, living in relationship is more like working with a compass, definitely not a method.

God doesn't want a perfect performance from me, he wants a relationship. He wants to be *with* me.[59]

So I am unraveling...back to my misconceptions, back to the place where I thought everything should be clear cut, back to my expectations of a check list for life.

The Point

A tree falls in the woods and there is no one around. No one to hear it. No one to see it.

Maybe it is a wood so thick and so large that the flowers growing on the forest floor are not seen by anyone. They are beautiful, but no one knows.

What is the point?

What is the point of a beautiful flower that no one will see? What is the point of a falling tree that no one will hear?

I often ask that question: What is the point? What is the point of what I do?

I very rarely have an answer to the myriad questions I ask.

Today, however, a light went on.

I love light. I love brightness and seeing and warmth and comfort. I love that Jesus says he is light. I know light, but I don't know God very well, so Jesus says, I am light.

Consider the sun. A daily visual analogy of God.

It is so very bright I cannot look directly at it. If I do it will blind me. It is too much for me, too much for my eyes.

I order my day by it. I cannot make it bend to my will, but I can bend to its. I can rise when it rises and benefit from the warmth, from being able to see better because of it.

I exist underneath it and I can submit to it. But I cannot

contain it, I cannot control it. It is so very much larger than me and marches according to its will, not mine.

It is beyond my reach, and yet it reaches to me. All that is good reaches me.

Jesus says, I am light. And what he's saying is, I created light to help you understand who I am.

Light.

And that is the answer to my question.

A flower grows in a wood so thick no one will ever see it. What is the point?

God.

God is the point. He designed the flower, not just its looks, but how it lives, how it grows, what environment it needs. And the flower is where it is at the pleasure of God.

And so am I.

God was pleased to think me up, create me, design me, make me look, work, feel, the way I do. I am where I am because it pleases him for me to be here.

And though no one may see me, no one may hear me, no one may acknowledge me, that is not the point.

The point is and always will be God.

Why Would Anyone Choose Comedy?

Jesus used lots of stories to help us understand the things of heaven. Like the story of the pearl of great price.

A man collected pearls and one day he came across the largest and most beautiful pearl he had ever seen, and he sold *everything* he had to buy that pearl.

Jesus says that's what the kingdom of heaven is like. Wanting him more than anything else, more than *everything* else.

We must choose, but how do we choose? It seems so hard to have to let go of everything else.

Diet and exercise

Those words are very familiar and very unpopular.

Few of us wants to go on a diet: restricting the quantity and content of our food consumption.

Few of us wants to add more energy expending activities to the day, my days are full enough as they are Thank you!

But diet and exercise are the prescriptions doctors give when we are overweight and our health begins to be adversely affected.

Larry knew he needed to go on a diet and add exercise.

But there were things he really, really, really enjoyed.

Things like Little Debbie Swiss Rolls. They come packaged in twos, a box of *twelve* packaged in twos. Inexpensive, they were a go to staple for our sweet tooth. Little Debbie's and a gallon of milk.

Other things too, like, Oreos, ice cream, candy bars, and much more.

And he liked sitting. After a hard day of work, standing all day, walking around his store, he liked to come home and *not* move.

Larry and I danced around healthier living for about 20 years. We got a lot of cutting-edge education about food and healthy eating from his employer. I would implement what I could, change a few things here and there.

But for the most part Larry wasn't budging. His thought was, Let me enjoy my life and that includes eating what I want. If my life is shorter, well at least I'll die happy with a Little Debbie's Swiss Roll in one hand.

I made incremental changes to our shopping and eating habits. Not that you could tell. But to make any more drastic changes was too overwhelming, too difficult. It required too much sacrifice. And while we intellectually understood the health benefits, they didn't motivate us to change.

Eventually Larry was diagnosed with high blood pressure and his doctor recommended diet and exercise. So we tried.

It was a lovely night. We had finished dinner and I suggested a walk. For everyone's sake, ours, the dog's, we all needed the exercise.

We started down the street and headed for the park. It really was a beautiful evening. It had rained earlier and was now warm and sunny. The best of June.

We paused at the end of the block to let two young neighbors pet the dog. Then we moved on.

The park would have several softball games going on, I knew Larry would want to stop and watch. We selected a small set of bleachers behind home plate. Only one other person was on those bleachers and the dog was able to sit on the ground.

We watched several innings. Larry was whistling a song he had played before we left home. Mocha was up and down the three bleacher seats checking everything out. Occasionally she would sit at my feet.

And then.

And then one of the players approached Mocha, unseen by me until he spoke, "Well you look like a nice..."

Mocha's hackles went up and she began jumping against the short leash I had her on...*snapping.* She wanted to bite him! As I grabbed for her collar, her would be admirer realized his mistake and backed away.

I was stunned. Apologetic. Mocha, now subdued, sat quietly looking at me.

Time to move on, I think.

So we did.

As we approached the fire station at the edge of the park Mocha had to poop.

This, at least, I was prepared for. Or so I thought. I took the plastic grocery bag I brought from home out of my pocket and waited for her to finish. But I was not prepared for what would happen next.

Some of her poop was dangling from her bottom, and she freaked, absolutely freaked. She began spinning in circles, rubbing against the sidewalk, smearing poop everywhere.

I picked up what I could, but she continued her frenzied dance across the street, out of control, panicked by a small piece of poop hanging by a thread. We couldn't save her, we couldn't stop her. She was being driven wild by her own poop.

Now I was laughing so hard I couldn't walk, I couldn't talk. And I could no longer control my bladder.

We reached the main road and I was chagrined by the idea of walking home down a main street, with my crazy dog, having just peed my pants.

As we rounded the final block toward home, we reflected on the turns our quiet evening walk had taken.

"This is supposed to be helping my blood pressure," Larry observed. "But by the time I go back to the doctor it will be up ten points. He'll ask me, 'What have you been doing?' And I'll say exactly what you told me to do: diet and exercise.

"I'm angry all the time because I can't eat what I want, and I'm stressed every day because I take the dog for a walk."

Diet and exercise are supposed to bring him good health, but it's making his life miserable, why would he do it?

CHOOSING COMEDY

Barn Chores

My friend, The Horse Whisperer, and I have been meeting
for breakfast once a week for nearly 20 years. She initiated it
as a way to get to know each other better and it has become a
highlight of my week.

Depending on what day we meet for breakfast she may be
heading out to the barn. Deb has a horse, named Tess. Tess is
boarded at a barn not very close to where Deb lives. So she
has quite a commute to go out and see, care for, and ride
Tess. The barn is a co-op which means everyone whose horse
boards there shares in the chores.

The chores on Thursday include filling baggies with food for
Tess's morning and evening meals for the coming week. Then
she must clean out Tess's stall, fill her water bucket, and if
someone is around, she will ride which entails getting Tess all
rigged up with bridle and reins, blanket and saddle, etc.

On Tuesdays Deb feeds and waters ALL the horses, then gets
Tess all rigged up and takes a lesson, afterward unrigging Tess
and cleaning her stall.

She does this when it is 98 degrees and 91 percent humidity,
and she does it when it is 20 degrees and the water buckets
are ice and must be chipped away. And she does it in all the
weather in between.

I cannot imagine doing those chores. It makes me tired (and
sweaty or shivering) just to hear her describe what awaits her,
after her 30-minute commute. The chores seem cumbersome,
time consuming, and overwhelming. It sounds exhausting
and like the last thing I would want to have to do *every*
Tuesday and Thursday, for ever and ever.

Why would she sign up for that?

House Rules

When my kids would gather to play in the neighborhood, they often compared notes on their families. It went something like this:

> My dad sells car parts.
>
> Well my dad guards banks.
>
> We just watched this show on TV.
>
> We're not allowed to watch TV.
>
> Wait, what?! You can't watch TV? Well it stinks to be you, doesn't it?

Sometimes what is normal to one family seems crazy and outrageous to another family.

God's kids like to talk about the House Rules too.

Most folks are familiar with the Ten Commandments, the ten laws for living God handed down to Moses after leading the Hebrews to freedom from Egyptian slavery.

These were the "house rules." God was letting the Hebrews know, you're my people, this is how we live.

Jesus invites everyone who is weary and tired from burdens too heavy to carry to come to him. He says his "yoke" is easy, and his burden is light.[60]
What is his yoke? A yoke is used to team up a pair of oxen or

horses to work together to pull a plow or cart. His yoke is a metaphor. He has paired up the two most important commandments from God: Love the Lord your God with all your heart, soul, strength and mind; and love your neighbor as yourself.

Love God, Love Others.

Sounds easy till you get to the fine print...Who is my neighbor?

Everybody.

Really. Everybody. No exceptions.

What does it mean to "love" them? Be patient with them, and kind to them. Don't be jealous of them, don't boast. Don't be proud, don't be rude, don't be selfish. Don't have a short fuse. Don't keep track of what everyone else did wrong. Don't gloat over the bad stuff others do. Delight in truth. Bear with everyone. Trust. Hope. Endure.[61]

That seems heavy to me.

God's kids like to talk about the House Rules and try to get others to follow them. But to those who aren't familiar they can seem crazy or outrageous.

They're awfully restrictive and seem to be a lot of work.

Why would anyone choose that?

Richard, Andy and Dianna

A few years after our failed attempt at Diet and Exercise

171

something happened. Our firstborn got married and soon after had two sons, and later a daughter. We are now grandparents.

What a wonderful thing! Tiny little people we get to hug and love and call George if we want. As they have grown, from babies to toddlers to preschoolers, we have been able to engage in their world more and more.

My husband cherishes memories of his grandfather, watching him in his workshop, learning about tools and repairs. He is eager to make similar memories with our grandchildren.

One day Larry came to me and said, "We are starting a life change on February 1." No discussion. Cold turkey we cut out sugar, grains, dairy, legumes. Two days in we experienced a really tough headache from sugar withdrawal.

After that he began noticing various aches and pains had subsided. He didn't snore anymore, and the weight began to fall away.

After four months he had lost 40 pounds. He says it was the easiest thing he has ever done.

People who hear how he did it - eliminating all those foods - are skeptical. That doesn't sound easy to them.

But for Larry it was a breeze, a walk in the park without threads!

Larry made what seemed to be a *drastic* life change gladly, *eagerly*. He did what seemed difficult for the love of Richard and Andy and Dianna.

Tess

I went to the barn with Deb recently. It wasn't the hottest day possible, but it was hot. It wasn't the biggest chore day, but there were chores. Deb worked up a really good sweat getting everything done. And then I watched Deb with Tess.

Horses are cool. They're like big doggies. My friend knows her horse. And loves her horse.

As I watched them rubbing noses, it warmed my heart. And a light went on.

My friend doesn't come to the barn to do chores. She comes to the barn to see her friend, a friend that she loves: Tess.

Deb does barn chores for the love of Tess.

For the Love of What?

What do I value above all else? For a while Larry valued Little Debbie's above good health.

But then along came three Pearls of Great Price and he valued time with them more and so all the things he thought were important, paled in comparison.

I was made to be in relation with God.

That relationship was broken when I chose something else above God. Before God, instead of God.

Jesus invites me...take up my cross and follow him.

It's hard, it means dying to self, letting go of everything else.

It seems impossible, and not terribly enticing.

Yet, God has forgiven me everything.

Every lie I ever told. Every selfish move I ever made. Every angry, hurtful, mean, hateful thought I ever had. Every puffed up, arrogant, impatient judgement I ever issued. He has seen my entire life, seen not just the actions but the thoughts, the motives, the inside of me.

He has seen what I will not confess here.

And he has forgiven me.

All of it.

I am the monster at the end of the book. And I am forgiven!

Jesus paid it all!

Jesus offers eternal life, and this is eternal life: to know God and Jesus Christ whom God has sent.

I must choose, but how do I choose? It seems so hard.

For the love of God I will choose to love my neighbor and my enemy. For the love of God, I will allow him to transform me so I am like his son, my savior. I want to look just like him.

I love God.

I choose to follow for the Love of God.

Not the End

It's not a complete picture.

I don't have all the pieces.

I can't see everything, I'm not at the top of the Eiffel Tower, my perspective is limited.

But these are some glimpses, some of the glimpses I have had of God, and glimpses of things he has taught me along my way.

I want clean shoes. I want to be put back together, by the one who made me in the first place. I want to live in relationship like I was made to do.

I hope these stories are like salt. I hope they made you thirsty. Thirsty for the living water.

Jesus says something that really causes people to stumble, that really becomes a barrier for them. He says, "No one comes to the Father, except by me."[62]

Peter knew it. When others were walking away from Jesus because of his hard teaching Jesus asked, "Are you going to leave me too?"

Peter answered, "Where would we go? You are the only one with the words of life."[63]

And there it is. Jesus is the only way to God. The only name by which men are saved.[64]

The only way our chains get broken.

CHOOSING COMEDY

Why?

Because he's the only one who offers forgiveness. He's the only one who offers to pay my tickets. The only one who offers his clean shoes in exchange for my poop covered ones.

Jesus is the only way. That's what I've learned in all these scenes. I'm broken and I can't put it all back together. I don't know how it's supposed to go.

I've tried, unsuccessfully, to piece it together. To break free. To clean my shoes.

I can't.

And no one else has offered.

Just Jesus.

We are loved. We are valued. We are pursued by the one who dreamt us up, the one who knows us completely.

We are offered forgiveness, and healing, and reconciliation to God.

I'm accepting. I'm choosing comedy.

CHOOSING COMEDY

CHOOSING COMEDY

Notes

1. Johnston, Ian. Notes from English 366: Studies in Shakespeare. Malaspina University College (now Vancouver Island University) in British Columbia, Canada. www.siue.edu/~ejoy/eng208NotesOnComedyAndTragedy.htm Accessed February 2011.
2. Ibid.
3. Ibid.
4. See Mark 5:1-20
5. This idea came from Meissner, Susan. *Secrets of a Charmed Life.* Penguin, 2015. "I am only responsible for my own choices. I am choosing to tell my story, Kendra. Who listens to it is not my burden. Telling it is."
6. Patel, Dev, performer. *The Best Exotic Marigold Hotel.* Fox Searchlight Pictures, 2011.
7. See Genesis 2, 3
8. See Luke 2:8-10
9. Lewis, C.S. *The Great Divorce.* Harper, 2001. p. VIII
10. Rickman, Alan, performer. *Galaxy Quest.* DreamWorks Pictures, 1999.
11. Lerner, Alan Jay, book and lyrics. "Almost Like Being in Love." *Brigadoon.* Loewe, Frederick, music. Broadway, 1947.
12. Nash, Johnny. "I Can See Clearly Now." *I Can See Clearly Now.* Epic, 1972, Track 7.
13. Chambers, Oswald. *My Utmost for His Highest* Journal. Barbour Publishing, Inc. 2010.
14. Stone, Jon. *The Monster at the End of This Book: Starring Lovable, Furry Old Grover.* Little Golden Books, 1971.
15. Matthew 3:17
16. Matthew 17:5
17. Luke 10:38-42
18. John 17:3
19. Alabama. "I'm in a Hurry (And Don't Know Why)." *American Pride.* RCA, 1992, Track 5.

20. Luke 2:10-12 paraphrased.
21. Isaiah 49:15
22. See Luke 12:7
23. See Psalm 56:8
24. See Psalm 139
25. Isaiah 55:8,9
26. Moses' story begins in Exodus 2
27. James 4:13-15 *New American Standard Bible*. Lockman Foundation, 1995.
28. The Kingston Trio. "M.T.A." *College Concert*. Capitol Records, 1982, Track 0.
29. Groves, Sara. "Different Kinds of Happy." *Fireflies and Songs*. Fair Trade/Columbia/Integrity, 2009, Track 3.
30. Ibid.
31. www.thefreedictionary.com/chagrin Accessed June 2011
32. The Dixie Cups. "Chapel of Love." *Chapel of Love*. Red Bird Records, 1964. Track 1.
33. West, Matthew. "Hello, My Name Is." *Into the Light*. Sparrow, 2012. Track 2.
34. See John 19:38
35. See John 20
36. Richman-Abdou, Kelly. "Kintsugi: The Centuries-Old Art of Repairing Broken Pottery with Gold" www.mymodernmet.com/kintsugi-kintsukuroi/. Accessed September 2019.
37. John 20:25. Stern, David. *Complete Jewish Bible*. Jewish New Testament Publications, 1998.
38. Ibid. John 20:27
39. Ibid. John 20:28,29
40. See Matthew 14:22-33
41. See Matthew 16:24-26
42. *Terminator 2: Judgement Day*. Directed by James Cameron. TriStar Pictures, 1991.
43. Lewis, C.S. *The Great Divorce*. Harper, 2001.
44. See Romans 5:3-5

45. James 1:2-8. *Good News Translation.* The American Bible Society, 1976.
46. See Hebrews 11:1.
47. See Revelation 4:10,11.
48. See John 14:6.
49. See John 21 for the whole story, especially verse 21 "Lord, what about him?"
50. *Aladdin.* Directed by Ron Clements and John Musker. Walt Disney Pictures, 1992.
51. This is my paraphrase of Proverbs 3:5,6.
52. See Matthew 5:40
53. See Matthew 5:41
54. See Matthew 5:44
55. See Matthew 16:22,23
56. See Matthew 26:39
57. See Luke 23:34
58. See Matthew 28:19
59. I am indebted to Skye Jethani for his teaching on the idea of God wanting to be with us. Jethani, Akash. *With.* Thomas Nelson, 2011.
60. See Matthew 11:30
61. See I Corinthians 13:4-7
62. John 14:6
63. John 6:68
64. See Acts 4:12

Acknowledgements

Thank you, Doug, for giving me space to write. In a job of numbers, you gave me a chance to use words. This wouldn't exist without that space. Tyler did well to dub you Rabbi Yoda, I have learned so much, and I am covered in your dust.

Thank you, Carol, for not letting up. You are my oldest friend, the one who knows my whole story, I'm so grateful for you. I love you my heart sister.

Thank you, Tina, for being my friend and my writing buddy. This manuscript is better because of your fresh eyes and skill. I love you.

Thank you, Deb, we have chewed over much more than breakfast. You are my thinking partner, and I love you.

Larry, thank you. You are my safe place. You are the one who encourages me. You show me what unconditional love is. I love you and thank God for the gift of you.

But mostly I must thank you, God. You dreamt me up. You paint pictures on my mind. Thank you for loving me in my brokenness. Thank you for the golden repair. Thank you for clean shoes. I want to trust you more every day.

CHOOSING COMEDY

About the Author

Robin Troia Schmidt was born in Detroit, Michigan. Her family moved to Bay Village, a suburb of Cleveland, Ohio, when she was nine. She has been following Jesus since she heard about his offer of forgiveness through Young Life her freshman year of high school.

While studying journalism and art at Eastern Michigan University, Ypsilanti, Michigan, Robin met Larry Schmidt over comedy in the dining hall. They married in 1982. The Schmidt's have three adult children, three grandchildren and make their home in Redford, Michigan.

Made in the USA
Middletown, DE
29 September 2019